UNIT ORIGAMI

Multidimensional Transformations

By Tomoko Fusè

Japan Publications, Inc.

Published by JAPAN PUBLICATIONS, INC., Tokyo and New York

Distributors:
UNITED STATES: Kodansha International/USA, Ltd., through Farrar, Straus & Giroux, 19 Union Square West, New York, 10003. CANADA: Fitzhenry & Whiteside Ltd., 195 Allstate Parkway, Markham, Ontario, L3R 4T8. BRITISH ISLES: Premier Book Marketing Ltd., I Gower Street, London WC1E 6HA. EUROPEAN CONTINENT: European Book Service PBD, Strijkviertel 63, 3454 PK De Meern, The Netherlands. AUSTRALIA AND NEW ZEALAND: Bookwise International, 54 Crittenden Road, Findon, South Australia 5007. THE FAR EAST AND JAPAN: Japan Publications Trading Co., Ltd., 1–2–1, Sarugaku-cho, Chiyoda-ku, Tokyo 101.

First edition: October 1990

LCCC No. 89–63238
ISBN 0–87040–852–6

Printed in U.S.A.

Foreword

A Book to Widen the Circle of Friends

For a while I am going to talk big, as if I were truly knowledgeable. The concept of Gaea, or the Earth as an immense living organism, is currently widely discussed. Its origins can be traced back to the desire to uncover what distinguishes life from so-called inanimate matter and to research in this field by the Soviet biochemist Aleksandr Ivanovich Oparin. In recent years such study has accelerated; and, perhaps in a few decades, the scientists' dream of discovering the distinction will bring down the wall between life and matter as resoundingly as the Berlin wall collapsed in 1989. Or the event may take place even sooner.

But those of us who love origami already know that from the outset there is no difference between inanimate things and living creatures. All origami, from a *sambo*-style footed tray or a balloon to a crane or an iris blossom, are equivalent, lovable masterpieces.

My claim is not farfetched. As Kōshō Uchiyama taught, origami is a world in which everyone who represents things from single sheets of paper experiences the joy of being a creator.

Our bodies are composed of something like 50 trillion cells. In other words, each individual human being is actually a vast aggregate of life entities, only a part of which are capable of suffering, joy, anger, love, or aesthetic feelings.

The brain controls such spiritual activity. The most important component of the brain is a kind of cell called a neuron, which has threadlike extensions —like a tiny snail's antennae. These extensions, called axons, interconnect— almost as if holding hands—and disconnect, making possible accumulation and transmission of information. I have heard that the process resembles atoms' joining to form molecules or the on-off principle of the computer. Perhaps this makes clear the basis of the idea of no distinction between inanimate matter and life.

Unit origami too makes the operations of atoms or neurons easier to understand. Each origami unit is expressionless in itself but has insertions and pockets by means of which it can be connected with other units to produce amusing, beautiful, or odd forms.

Today scientists are busily creating wonderful new kinds of matter and life through biotechnology and hypertechnology and offering them to us in various forms. Is my amateur suggestion that unit origami can help solve problems of genetic combination, special environmental conditions, and the search for good catalysts unworthy of consideration?

Like a scientist, Tomoko Fusè fascinates us by creating, one after another, a startling number of new kinds of units. In principle, unit origami is simple. But merely endlessly connecting units with insertions and pockets is unexciting. Tomoko Fusè's strength lies in the way she is able to create unit-origami forms that are entertaining, lovely, and surprising. And her witty and skillful way of explaining her work is extremely winning.

In a very short time, she has published many fine books that have attracted larger numbers of people to unit origami. This is a great achievement.

On a more personal note, I have a son who is now twenty-one and a daughter who is ten. As I observe them day by day, it seems that my daughter is the wittier and more promising of the two. I am not intimating that my son is unreliable. I think he feels the same way I do.

And sometimes, my relation with Tomoko Fusè overlaps in my mind with the relation between my son and daughter. I actually look on her as both a promising younger sister and, at the same time, a rare good comrade.

Her generous efforts and devotion to the Gaea interpretation of the Earth have resulted in a book that I am certain will win still more people to origami. I hope that all of you will join me in the circle of origami friends who can now use her book as a catalyst as we intensify our devotion to this fascinating field.

Kunihiko Kasahara

Preface

Unit origami is a lucid kind of origami. It does take time, plenty of paper, and patience. But, after the units have been folded and assembled, the final forms are clear and convincing. The happiness they bring gradually changes to surprise at the kinds of things possible with origami. But perhaps I should begin with a few words of explanation for people who are new to this field.

As the name implies, unit origami is a method of producing various forms by assembling different numbers of prepared units. Hands and paper are the only things used to make the units: no scissors, compasses, glues, or other adhesives are needed.

Because no adhesives are used, sometimes assemblies are unstable, or finished forms are less than completely clean-cut owing to paper thickness. But this in no way detracts from the worth and interest of unit origami. Other factors account for the appeal of this kind of paper folding and assembly. First it is easy. Second, it has some of the fascination of a puzzle, But slowly, as one folds more and more of them, unit origami go beyond puzzles and reveal forms that exceed the folder's calculations. They develop in unexpected ways. In short, though lucid and exciting, unit origami have the extra attraction of being incalculable. I became entranced by unit origami precisely because of this incalculable quality and because of my desire to learn more about it.

Only one aspect of the wide and varied world of origami, unit origami is a new field that has developed in recent years and that still has many interesting possibilities to reveal.

All origami begins with putting the hands into motion. Understanding something intellectually and knowing the same thing tactilely are very different experiences. To learn origami, you must fold it. I shall be very glad if this book helps you make what might be called a hands-on acquaintance with this new origami world. I hope that, together, we can gain more and deeper knowledge about unit origami as we continue enjoying it.

This book is based on material from a unit-origami series published, in Japanese, in 1987 by the Chikuma Shobo Publishing Co., Ltd. Some new works have been added, the drawings have been altered in the interests of understandability, and the whole text has been rewritten.

Finally, I should like to express my gratitude to the people who helped make the publication of the book possible. First I offer gratitude to Iwao Yoshizaki, president of Japan Publications, Inc., and to Miss Yotsuko Watanabe, the editor, for their painstaking and careful efforts and for listening to my willful demands. In addition, I should like to thank Tatsundo Hayashi, who designed the cover; Kazuo Sugiyama, the photographer; and Richard L. Gage, the translator.

June 6, 1990   Tomoko Fusè

Contents

Chapter 4: The Equilateral Triangle Plus Alpha 103

Chapter 5: Growing Polyhedrons 133

Chapter 6: Simple Variations 167

Key to Directions

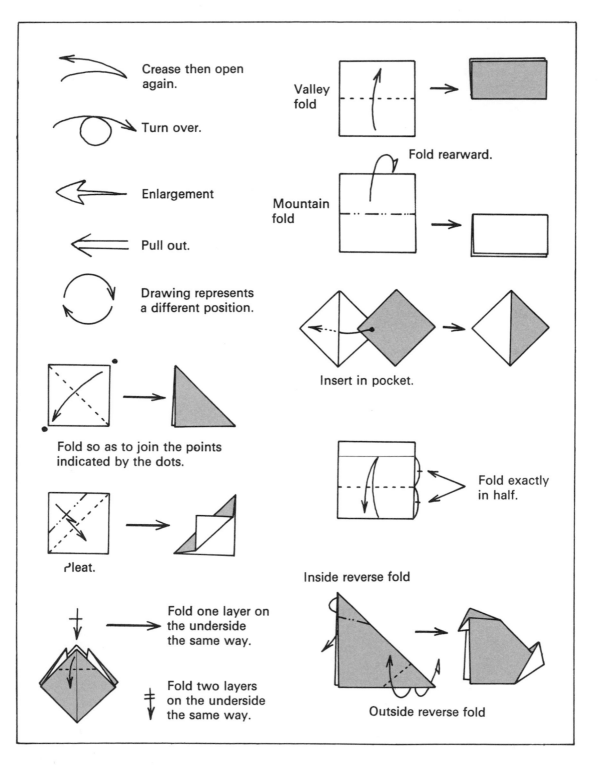

Crease then open again.

Turn over.

Enlargement

Pull out.

Drawing represents a different position.

Fold so as to join the points indicated by the dots.

Pleat.

Fold one layer on the underside the same way.

Fold two layers on the underside the same way.

Valley fold

Fold rearward.

Mountain fold

Insert in pocket.

Fold exactly in half.

Inside reverse fold

Outside reverse fold

▲ Open frame I (p. 62): 30-unit (left), 12-unit (middle), and 48-unit (right) assemblies

▼ Cube 6-unit assembly plus alpha (Axel's method; left), cube with pyramid added (middle; p. 74), and cube 12-unit assembly plus alpha (right; p. 82)

◀ Bird tetrahedron 3-unit assemblies connected by means of long- and short-joint materials (p. 144)

▼ Connecting 6 dual wedges (p. 164)

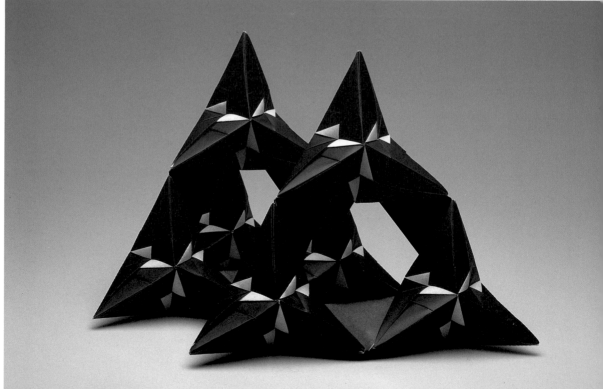

Pinwheel cube 6-unit assemblies
connected by means of Joint
No. 2 (p. 151)

Bird tetrahedron 3-unit
assemblies connected by
means of Joint No. 1 (p.
138)

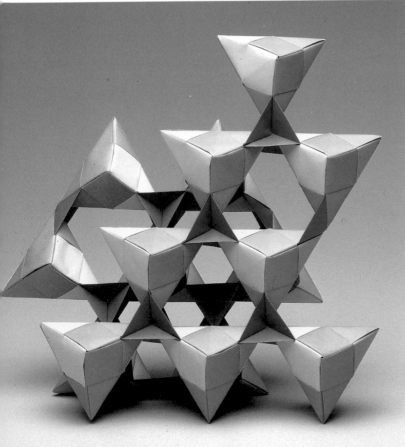

▲ Transformations of rhombicuboctahedron (pp. 210–217)

▼ Cuboctahedron and cube (p. 179)

Cuboctahedron
(left) and in-
termediary stage
of transformation
(right)

*Transformations of
Cuboctahedron*
(pp. 199–207)

Truncated
octahedron

Compound
cube and regular
octahedron

Regular
octahedron

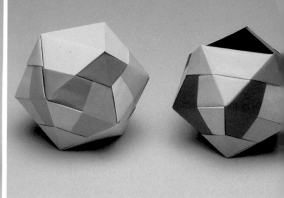

Regular icosahedron 12-unit assembly (left) and small dish (right; p. 38)

Regular icosahedron 14-unit assembly (left) and pot (right; p. 34)

Octagonal star 6-unit assembly (p. 48)

Snub cube (p. 68)

Open frame II—plain, 84-unit assembly (p. 65)

Open frame II—plain, 28-unit (left) and 25-unit (right) assemblies (p. 66)

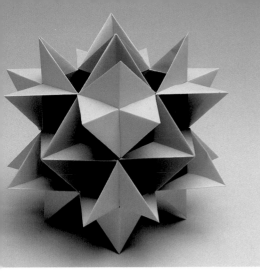

Simple Sonobè 12-unit assembly plus alpha (p. 80)

Little turtle 30-unit (left) and 6-unit (right) assemblies (p. 56)

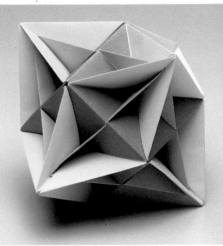

Muff (p. 172): 6-unit (left) and 12-unit (right) assemblies

Double-pocket 12-unit assembly plus alpha (p. 86)

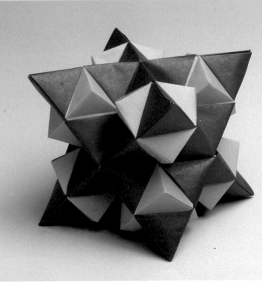

Equilateral triangles (p. 108)

Equilateral triangles (p. 104)

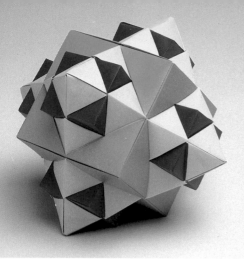

Square units (p. 100)

Square units (p. 101)

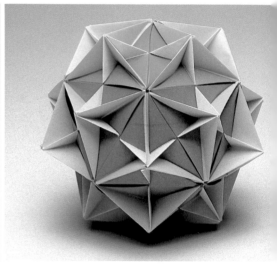

Propeller units (p. 123)

Propeller units (p. 123)

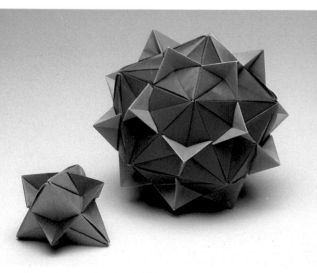

Propeller units (p. 118)

Dual triangles 30-unit concave assembly
(p. 131)

Chapter 1: Belt Series

In contrast to the traditional origami approach of combining 3 or 6 identical units to form a solid figure, this chapter explains ways of forming regular solid units (for instance, regular tetrahedrons [4 faces] and icosahedrons [20 faces]) by assembling beltlike strip units. In Japanese, these units are called *haramaki*. A *haramaki* is any of several kinds of sashes or protectors worn wrapped (*maki*) around the belly (*hara*) for protection or warmth.

Cube—Small Square-pattern Belt Unit

Belt Unit

First 2 units of paper are joined in a ring to form a squared loop frame. This is the belt. The pointed top and bottom units are then inserted to form a clean, sturdy cube with perfectly matched measurements.

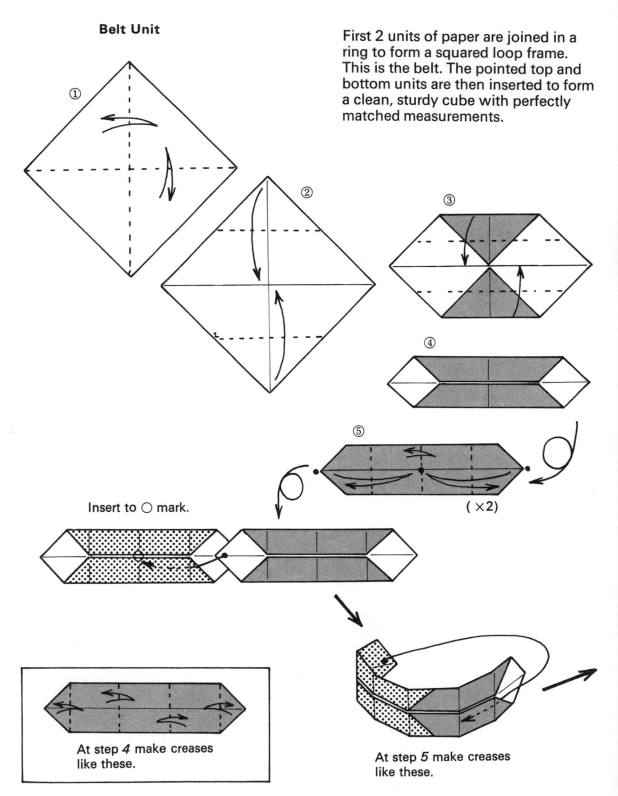

Insert to ○ mark.

(×2)

At step *4* make creases like these.

At step *5* make creases like these.

Top and Bottom Belt

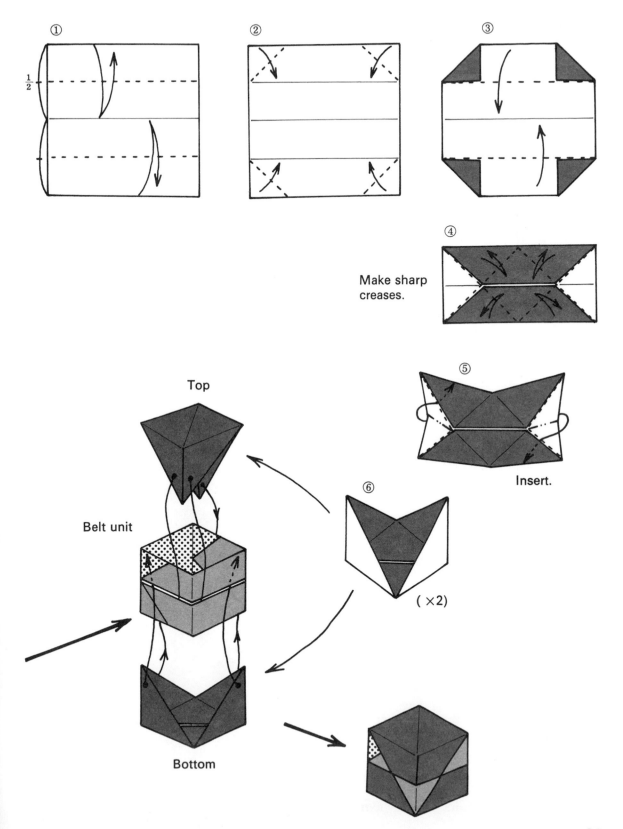

① $\frac{1}{2}$

②

③

④ Make sharp creases.

⑤ Insert.

⑥ (×2)

Top

Belt unit

Bottom

Cube—Large Square-pattern Belt Unit

Belt Unit

The assembly is the same as for the small square-pattern belt, but the folding method is simpler.

Both of these cubes make attractive small-gift containers. A small cake or piece of candy is all the more appetizing when offered in such an unusual container.

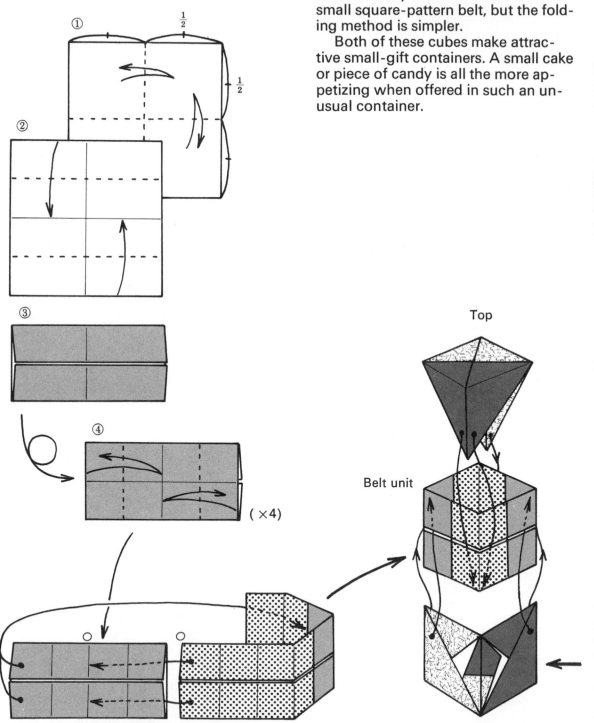

Assemble 4 into a square loop.

Cubes made from square-pattern belt units: small (left), with opened lid (middle), and large (right)

Top and Bottom Unit

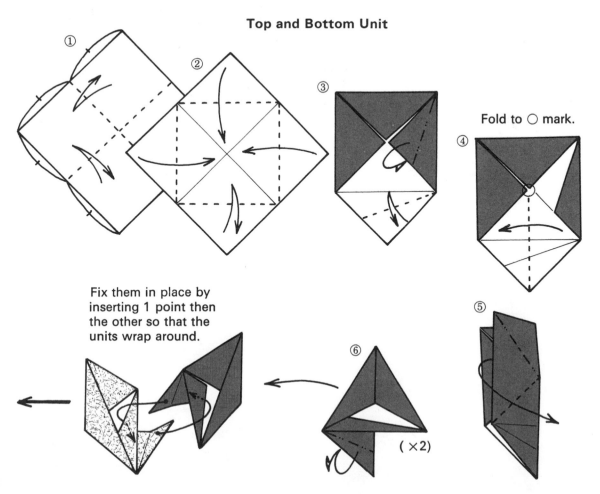

① ②

③ Fold to ○ mark.

④

Fix them in place by inserting 1 point then the other so that the units wrap around.

⑥ (×2)

⑤

Cube—Triangular-pattern Belt Unit (1 Point)

A cube may be produced by beginning with step *5* on p. 22, repositioning the folding lines, and connecting 3 units in a triangular loop. Making cubes from squares and triangles is stimulating fun. The bigger the units are, however, the weaker their joints.

Triangular-pattern belt unit (left) assembled in a cube (right)

Belt Unit

Make a crease like this figure.

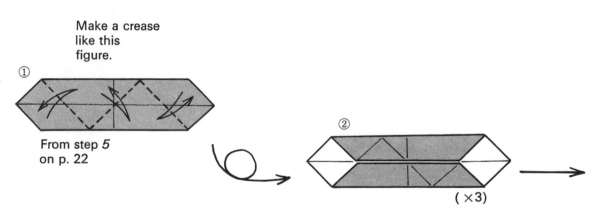

① From step *5* on p. 22

②

(×3)

Top and Bottom Unit

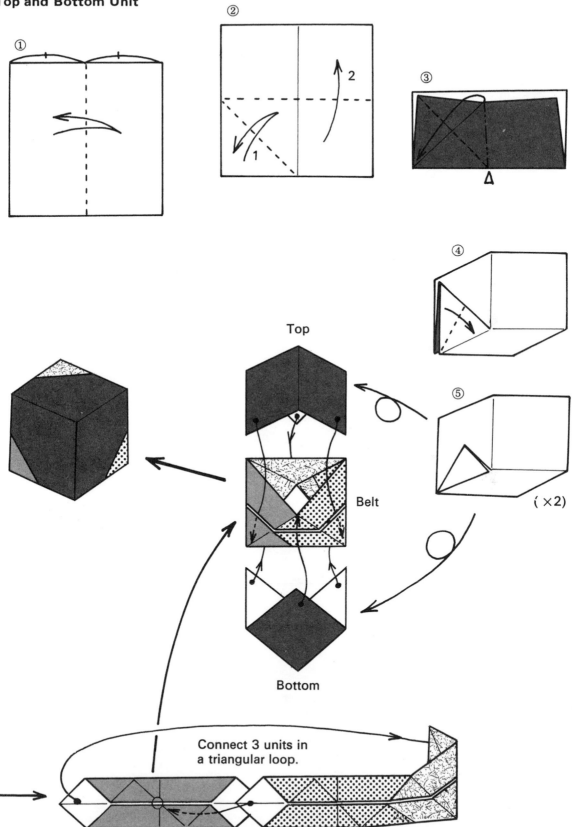

① ② ③ ④ ⑤ (×2)

Top

Belt

Bottom

Connect 3 units in
a triangular loop.

27

Small Regular Octahedron

Let us make a regular octahedron. Stopping folding before insertion of the top part of the belt unit results in a useful pen stand. A hooklike connection strengthens the bottom section (Fig. 1).

Belt Unit

①

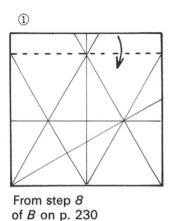

From step *8*
of *B* on p. 230

②

③

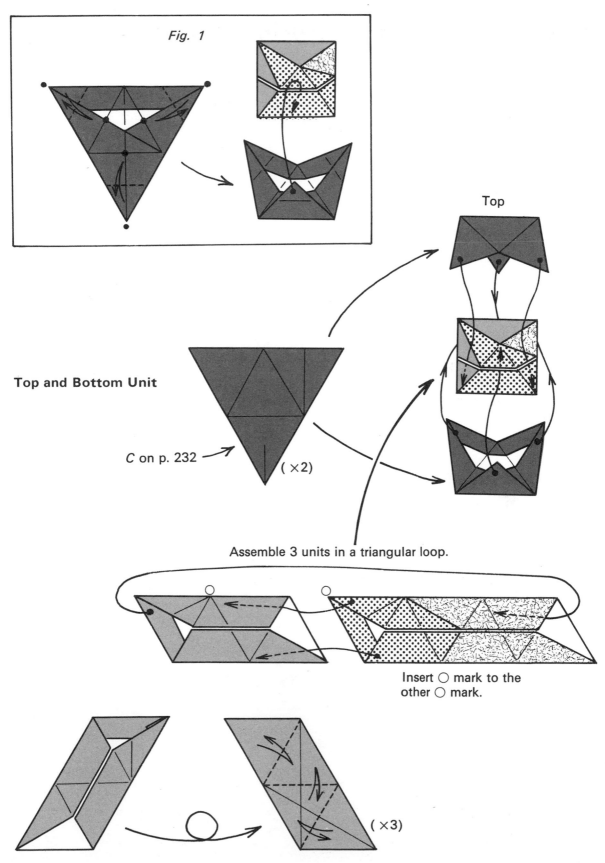

Fig. 1

Top

Top and Bottom Unit

C on p. 232 (×2)

Assemble 3 units in a triangular loop.

Insert ○ mark to the
other ○ mark.

(×3)

Icosahedron (15 Units)—Pavilion

To make an icosahedron, add a pentagonal lid to a 5-unit belt assembly. The connection will be firm if one end of the belt is left open as shown in the figure. It may be left as a regular octahedron, as shown in step *1*.

Top and Bottom Unit

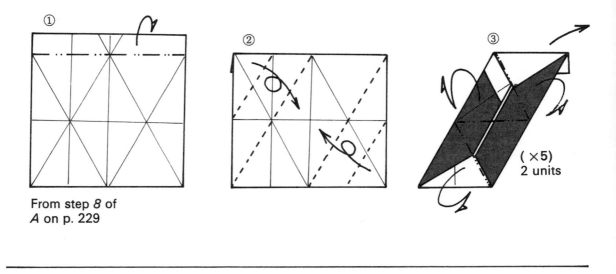

① From step *8* of *A* on p. 229

③ (×5) 2 units

Belt Unit

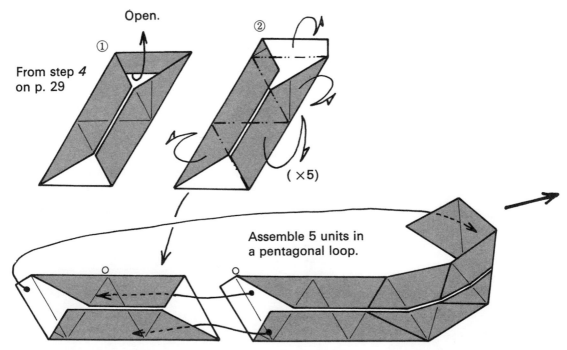

① From step *4* on p. 29

Open.

(×5)

Assemble 5 units in a pentagonal loop.

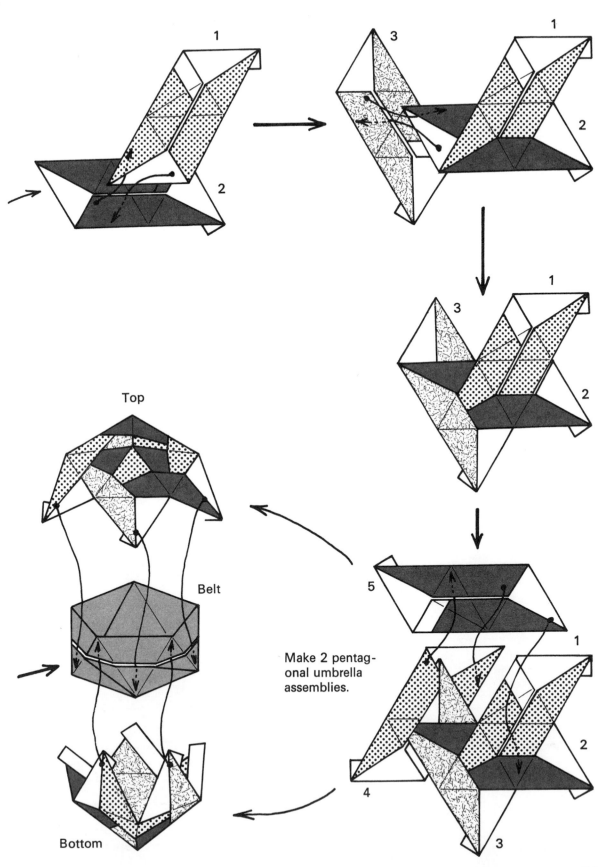

Top

Belt

Make 2 pentagonal umbrella assemblies.

Bottom

Various Pentagonal Umbrellas

A

①

From step *8* of *B*
on p. 229

Combining the belt unit with the top umbrella assembly alone produces something reminiscent of the kinds of pavilions built for world fairs or the kinds of tents used for bazaars and circuses.

Using the belt unit and the pentagonal umbrella assembly in this section as reference, design your own amusing and interesting pavilions.

②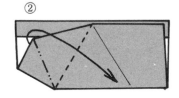

(×5)

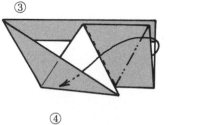

B

①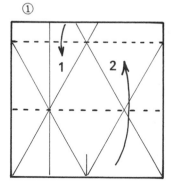

1   2

Begin with step *7* of *A* folded from the 1″ crease on p. 228.

②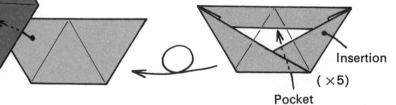

③

④

Insertion

(×5)

Pocket

32

Variation of pavilion (left) and regular icosahedron 15-unit assembly (right)

C

①

From step *2* of *B*

② (×5)

Insert between these 2.

Insert into the uppermost layer.

Insertion

Pocket

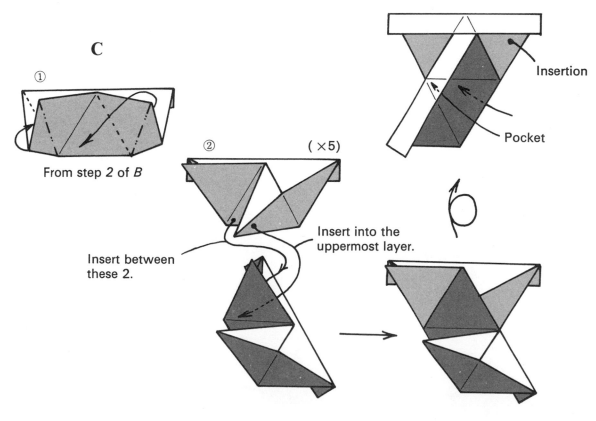

Regular Icosahedron (14 Units)—Pot

The upper half of the belt unit is made of 3 large units composed of an assembly of 2 kinds of smaller units. Using the reverse folds shown on p. 36 to produce the lower half results in a pot-shaped belt unit. Employing reverse folds eliminates unwanted excess on the surfaces.

Skill and experience are needed to make this 14-unit assembly, which is difficult to assemble and comes apart easily.

Belt Unit (upper half)

From step *8* of *B*
on p. 230

From the reverse fold
of *B* on p. 231

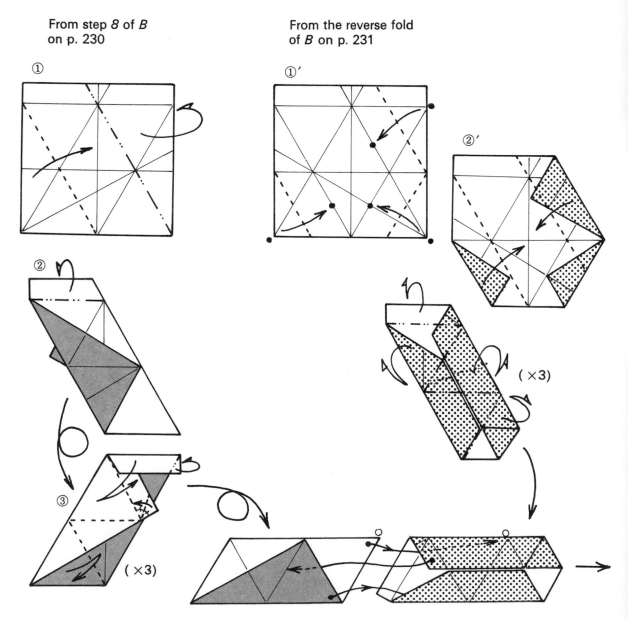

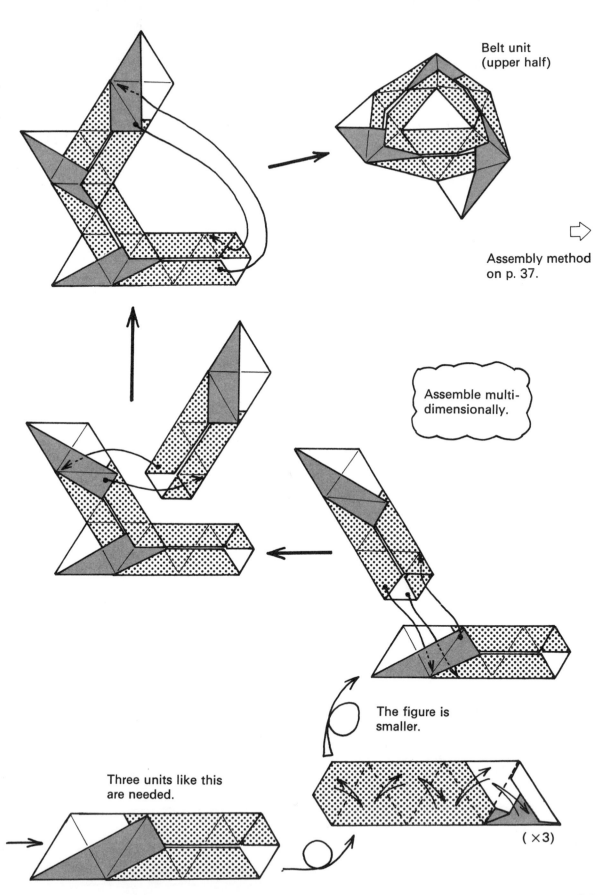

Belt unit
(upper half)

Assembly method
on p. 37.

Assemble multi-
dimensionally.

The figure is
smaller.

Three units like this
are needed.

(×3)

Belt Unit (lower half)

From the reverse fold
of *B* on p. 231

From step *8* of *B*
on p. 230

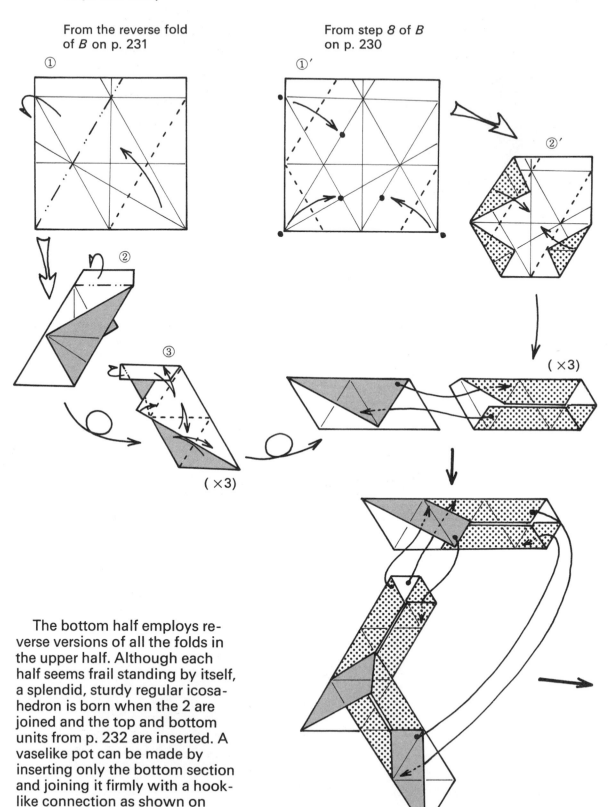

The bottom half employs reverse versions of all the folds in the upper half. Although each half seems frail standing by itself, a splendid, sturdy regular icosahedron is born when the 2 are joined and the top and bottom units from p. 232 are inserted. A vaselike pot can be made by inserting only the bottom section and joining it firmly with a hooklike connection as shown on p. 29.

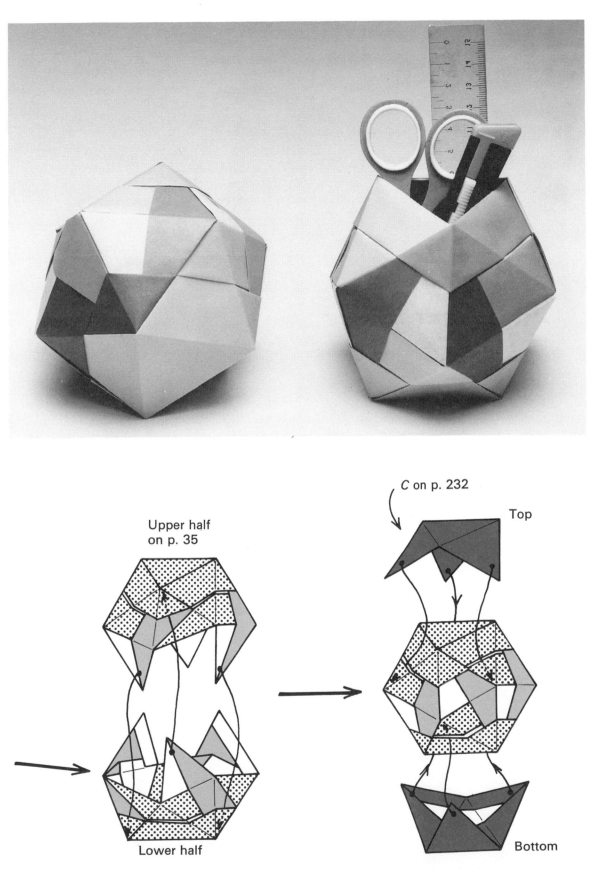

Upper half
on p. 35

C on p. 232

Top

Lower half

Bottom

Regular Icosahedron (12 Units) —Small Dishes

Unit a

①

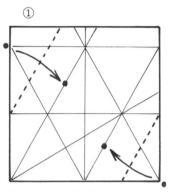

From step *8* of *B*
on p. 230

The dish made from half of the 14-unit assembly on p. 34 is very interesting. Slight alterations in its folds change its shape. Of course joining 2 of them produces a regular icosahedron. Although it is a departure from the belt-unit theme, I include it in this chapter because it is related to 14-unit assemblies.

②

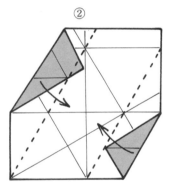

Two unit types (*a* and *b*) are combined.

③

④

Fold rearward.

⑤ ⑥

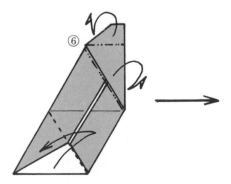

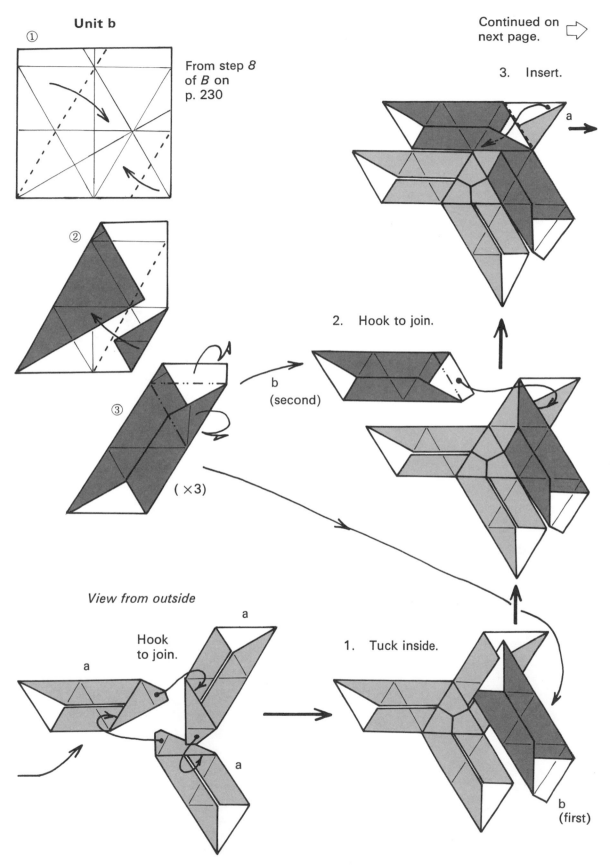

Unit b

Continued on next page. ⇨

① From step *8* of *B* on p. 230

3. Insert.

a →

②

③

b (second)

2. Hook to join.

(×3)

View from outside

a

Hook to join.

a

a

1. Tuck inside.

b (first)

39

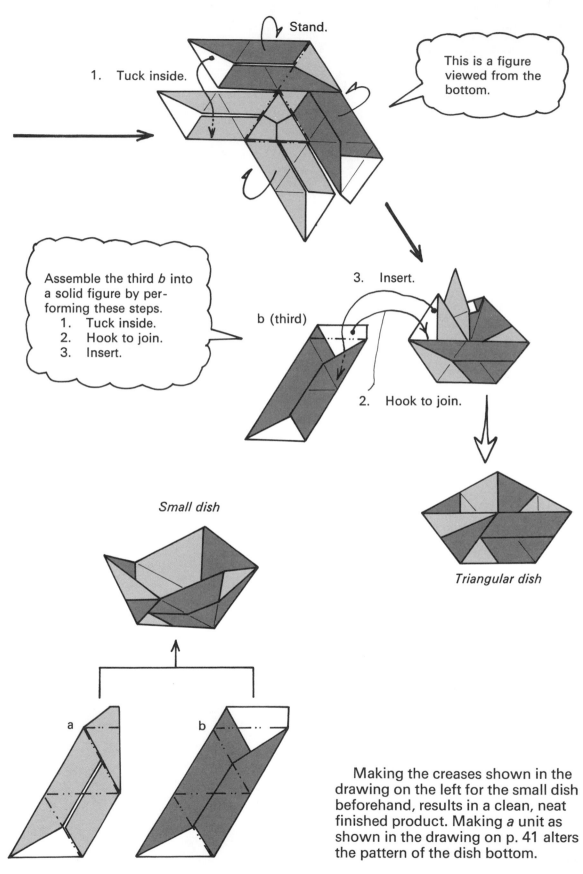

Stand.

1. Tuck inside.

This is a figure viewed from the bottom.

Assemble the third *b* into a solid figure by performing these steps.
1. Tuck inside.
2. Hook to join.
3. Insert.

3. Insert.

b (third)

2. Hook to join.

Small dish

Triangular dish

a

b

Making the creases shown in the drawing on the left for the small dish beforehand, results in a clean, neat finished product. Making *a* unit as shown in the drawing on p. 41 alters the pattern of the dish bottom.

40

Triangular dishes (2 on the left) and small dishes (2 on the right)

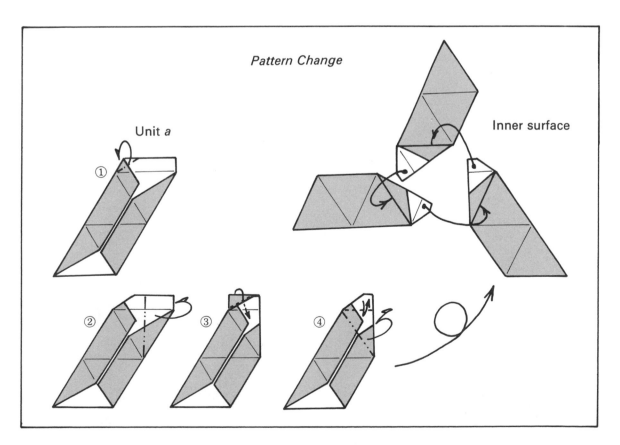

Pattern Change

Unit *a*

Inner surface

①

②

③

④

Regular Icosahedron Made with 2 Small Dishes

Joining 2 small dishes produces a regular icosa-hedron. As in the case of the 14-unit assembly, the lower half must be folded on creases that are the reverse of those used in the upper half. While making these, I was amused and entertained at the way the triangular fold becomes a dish and 2 dishes join to make an icosahedron.

Make reverse fold of unit *a* on p. 38.

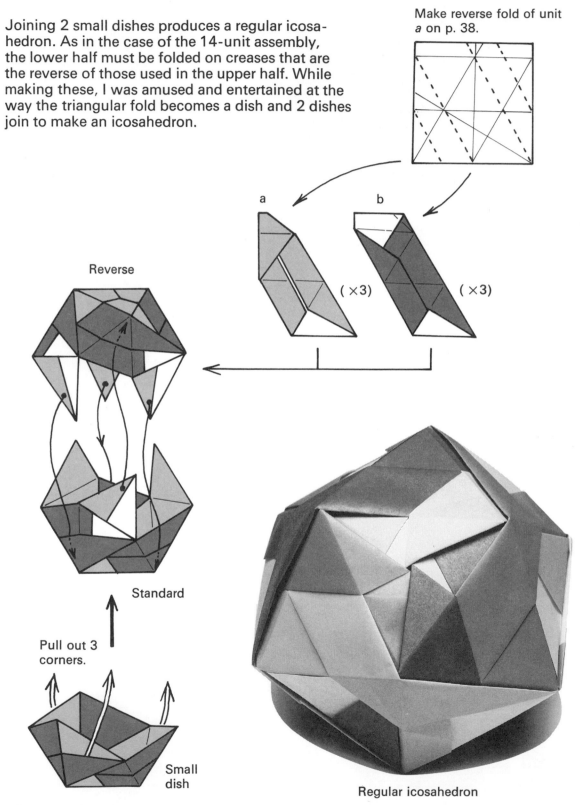

a

b

(×3)   (×3)

Reverse

Standard

Pull out 3 corners.

Small dish

Regular icosahedron

Double Wedges

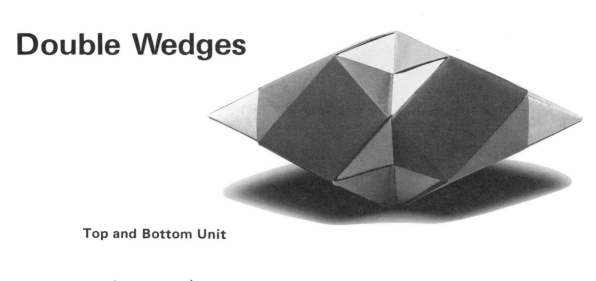

Top and Bottom Unit

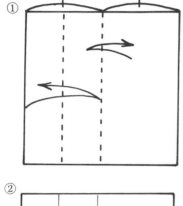

①

The last in the belt series is this interesting fold, both ends of which are narrowed in wedgelike shapes. Aside from altered folding lines, it is exactly like the solid belt-form figure on p. 22.

Continued on next page. ⇨

②

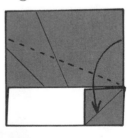

⑥

③

④

⑤

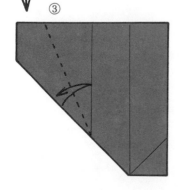

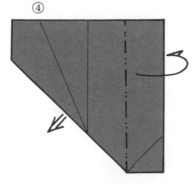

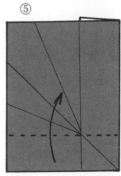

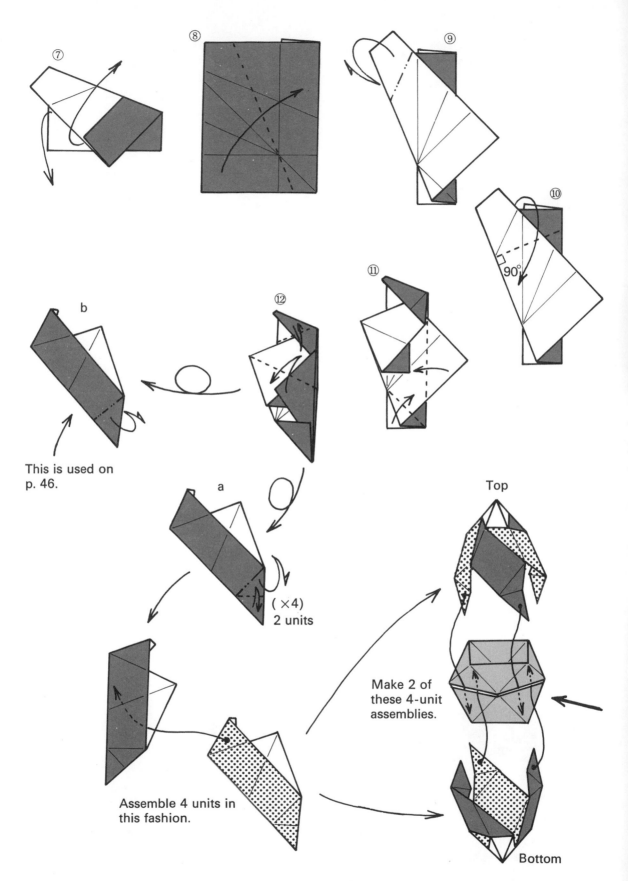

⑦

⑧

⑨

⑩

90°

⑪

⑫

b

This is used on
p. 46.

a

(×4)
2 units

Make 2 of
these 4-unit
assemblies.

Top

Assemble 4 units in
this fashion.

Bottom

Belt Unit

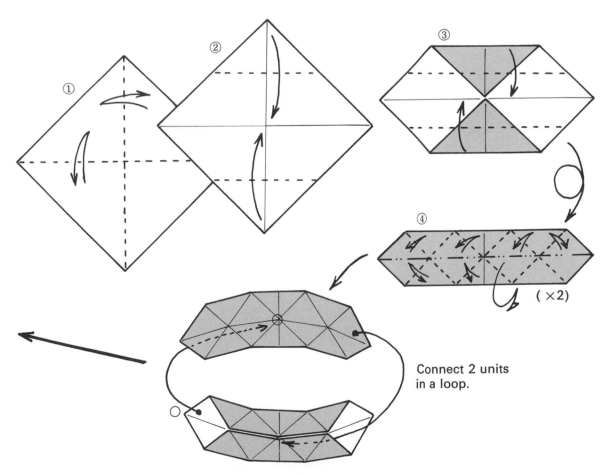

Connect 2 units
in a loop.

(×2)

Reverse-fold Double Wedge

Reverse fold

By means of reverse folding, it is possible to make the double wedge without a belt form. Work out ways to assemble more units by altering the folding lines.

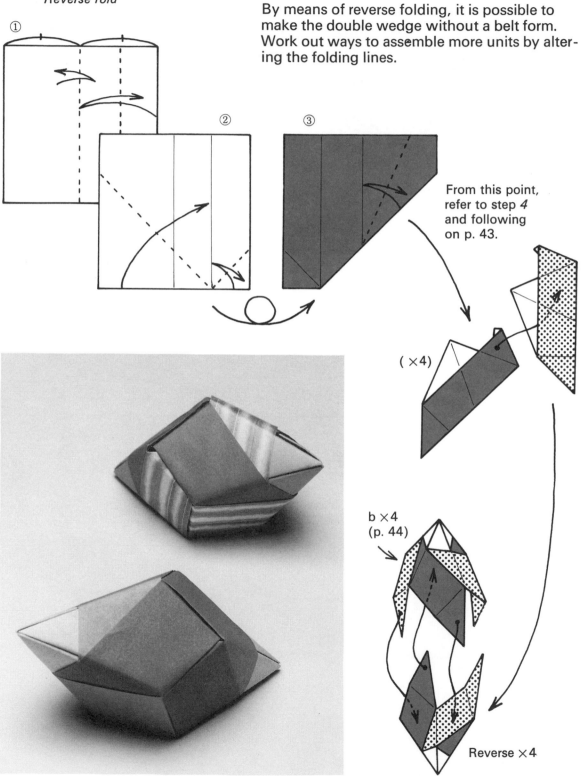

From this point, refer to step *4* and following on p. 43.

(×4)

b ×4
(p. 44)

Reverse ×4

Chapter 2: Windowed Series

In this chapter, I introduce polyhedrons that, instead of being tightly closed, have windowlike openings for ventilation and that, because they can be seen through, remind me of space stations.

Octagonal Star

As this origami shows, such units may be assembled with or without windows. Multistage, regular folding produces handsome and elaborate forms. Once you understand the folding method, you can deviate from the instructions to devise other methods that you find easy to work with. Joint materials are folded to take the place of adhesives in connecting basic units; that is, stars.

Octagonal star 6-unit assembly without windows (left) and the same figure with windows (right)

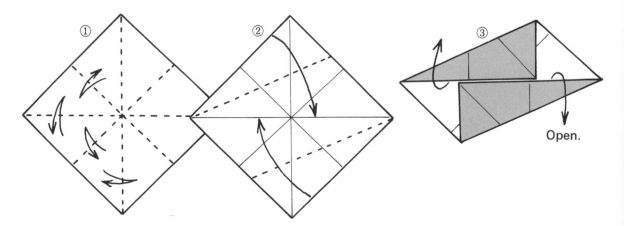

Open.

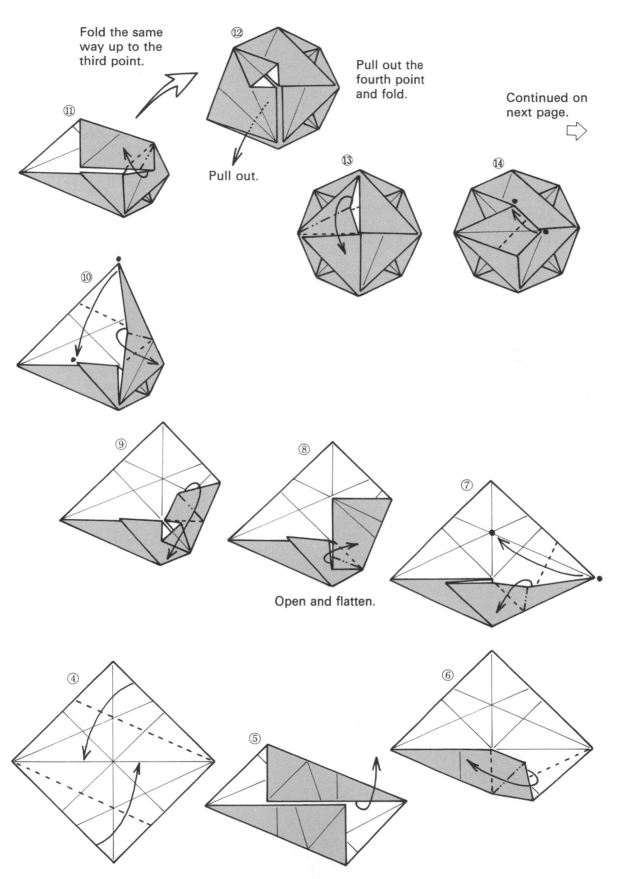

Fold the same way up to the third point.

⑫ Pull out.

Pull out the fourth point and fold.

Continued on next page.

⑪

⑬

⑭

⑩

⑨

⑧

Open and flatten.

⑦

④

⑤

⑥

49

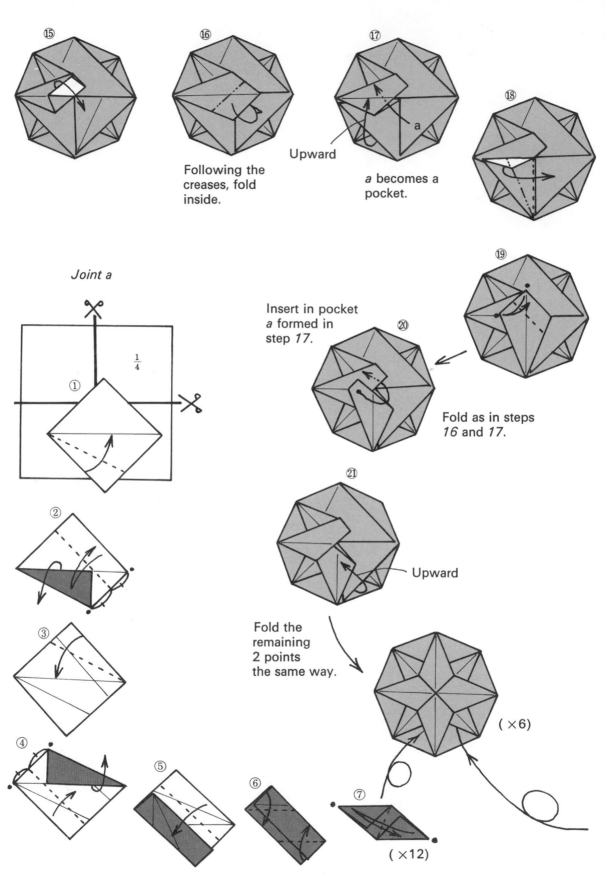

⑮ ⑯ ⑰ ⑱

Following the
creases, fold
inside.

Upward

a becomes a
pocket.

Joint a

¼

①

Insert in pocket
a formed in
step *17*.

⑲

⑳

Fold as in steps
16 and *17*.

②

③

⑳

Upward

Fold the
remaining
2 points
the same way.

(×6)

④

⑤

⑥

⑦

(×12)

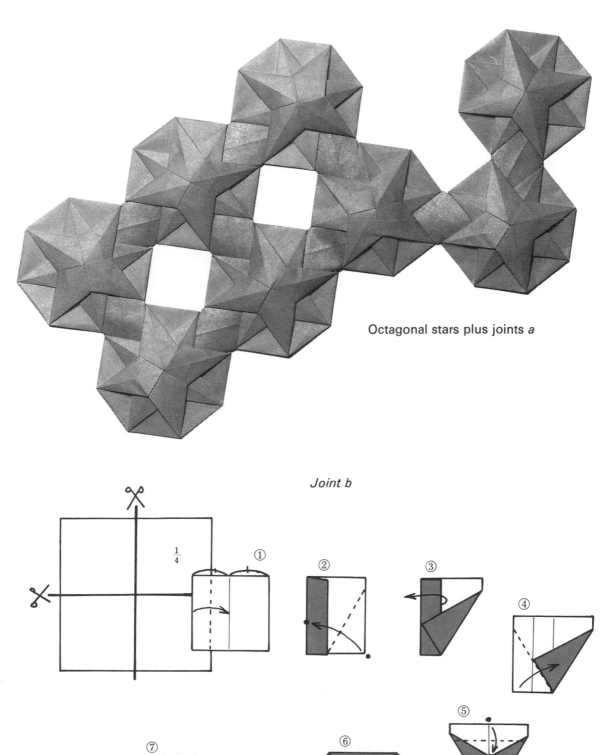

Octagonal stars plus joints *a*

Joint b

①   ②   ③   ④   ⑤

⑥ Tuck inside.

⑦ (×8)

$\frac{1}{4}$

Hexagonal Star

Although, as is the case with the octagonal star, the joints in this figure are slightly weak, its patterns are appealing whether it is assembled in solid or plane form.

Try devising joints other than the ones shown here.

Begin with step 7 of A folded from the 1'' crease on p. 228.

Hexagonal star 4-unit assembly with joints *a* (×6) and joints *b* (×4)

①

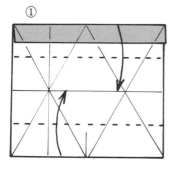

②

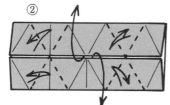

After creasing, reopen.

③

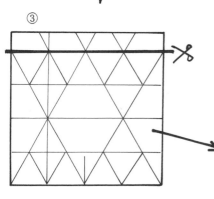

Make creases.

④

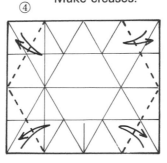

⑤

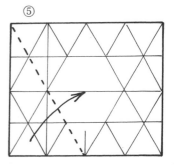

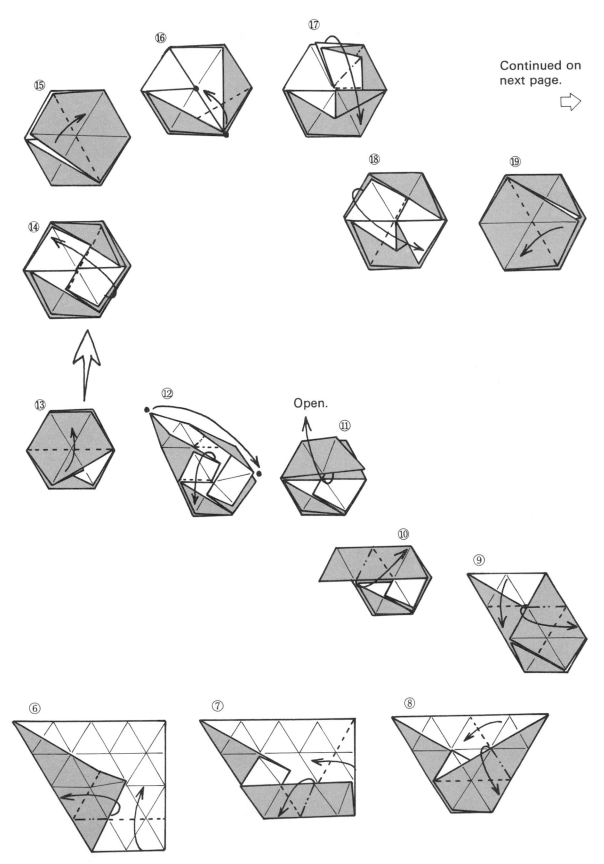

⑮ ⑯ ⑰

Continued on
next page.
⇨

⑱ ⑲

⑭

⑬ ⑫ Open. ⑪

⑩ ⑨

⑥ ⑦ ⑧

53

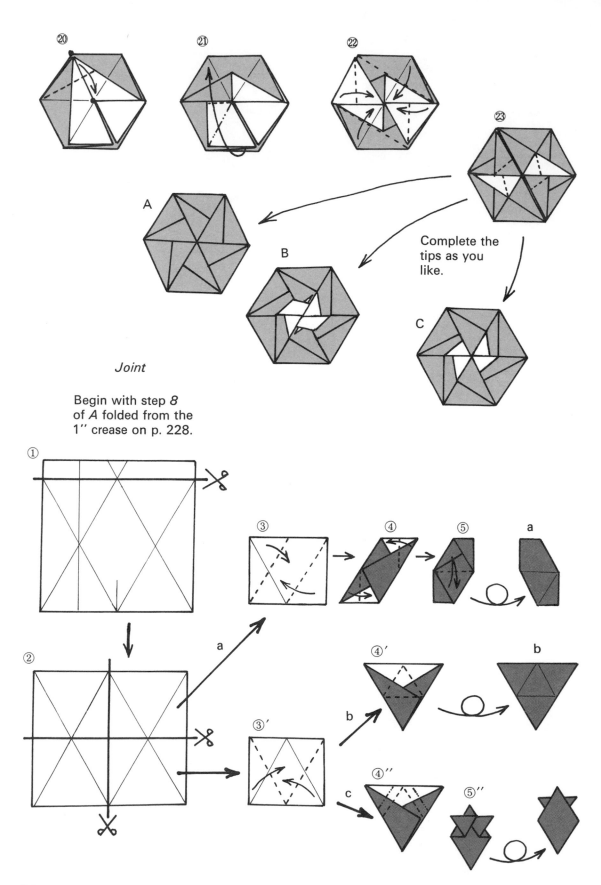

㉑ ㉒ ㉓

A

B

Complete the
tips as you
like.

C

Joint

Begin with step *8*
of *A* folded from the
1″ crease on p. 228.

①

②

③ ④ ⑤ a

③′

④′ b

c ④″ ⑤″

Hexagonal stars
connected in a plane

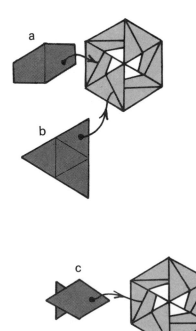

Snowflakes made from joints *c*

Little Turtle

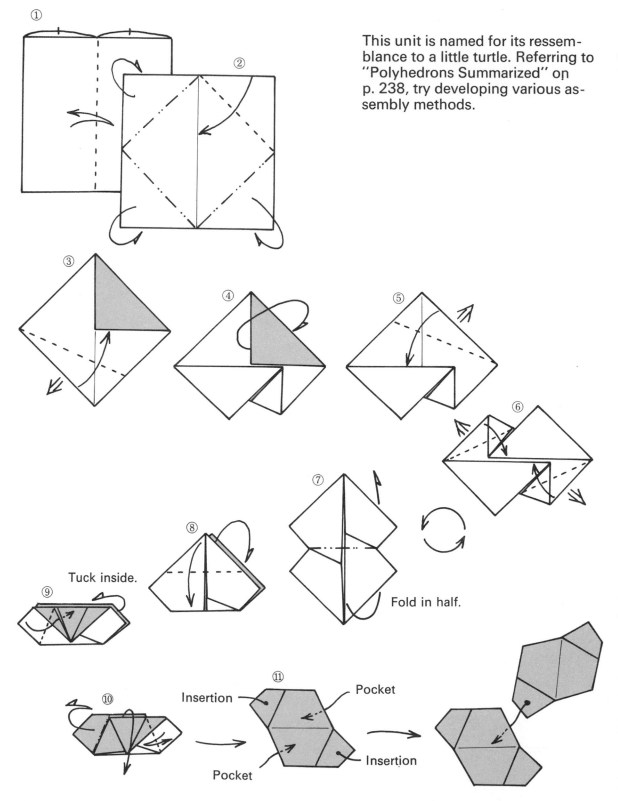

This unit is named for its ressemblance to a little turtle. Referring to "Polyhedrons Summarized" on p. 238, try developing various assembly methods.

Tuck inside.

Fold in half.

Insertion

Pocket

Pocket

Insertion

Assemblies of 12 (left), 4 (middle), and 24 (right) units

Assemblies of 6 (left) and 30 (right) units

Pyramid

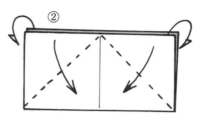

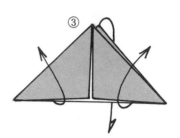

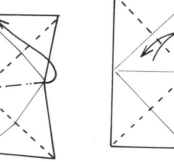

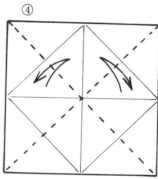

Assemble on the creases.

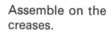

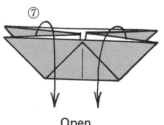

Open.

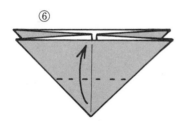

Intermediary form

Stand the triangle up.

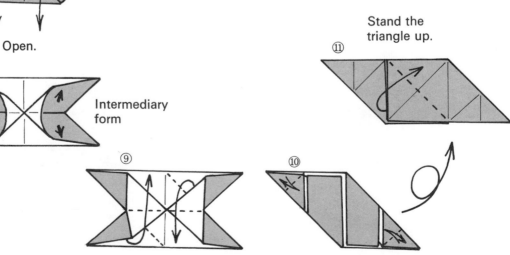

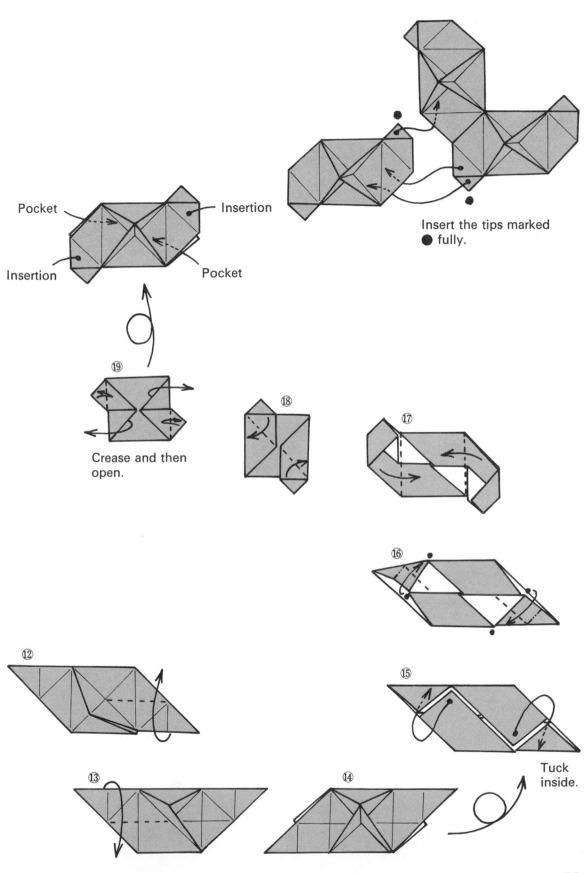

Pocket

Insertion

Insertion

Pocket

Insert the tips marked ● fully.

⑲

Crease and then open.

⑱

⑰

⑯

⑫

⑮

Tuck inside.

⑬

⑭

59

The 2 large forms (top and middle) are both 12-unit assemblies. The small form (bottom left) is a 6-unit assembly.

Assemble in such a way as to make triangular or square windows. Because they are not very sturdy, use fairly stiff paper about 4 inches (10 centimeters) to a side. As is seen in the photograph above, 12-unit assemblies can produce different finished forms.

Closing the Windows

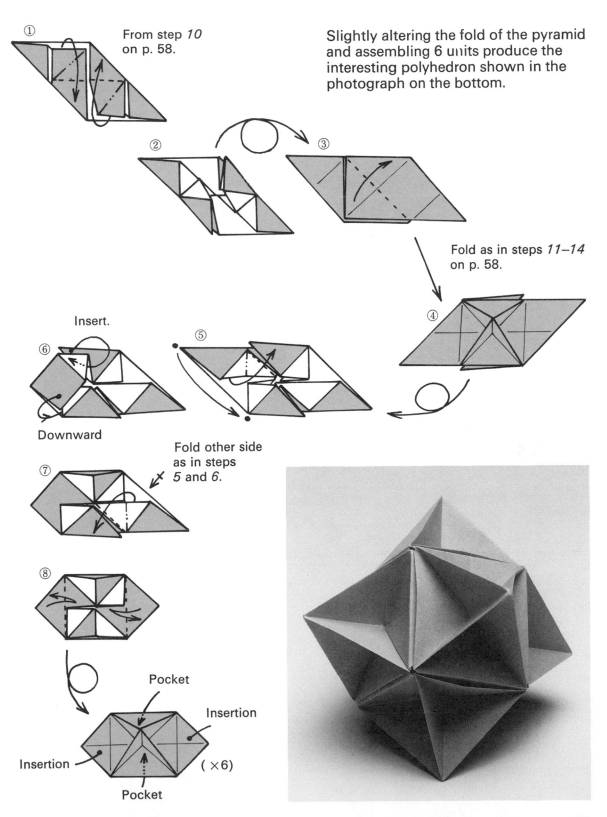

① From step *10* on p. 58.

Slightly altering the fold of the pyramid and assembling 6 units produce the interesting polyhedron shown in the photograph on the bottom.

②

③

Fold as in steps *11–14* on p. 58.

④

Insert.

⑥

Downward

⑤

Fold other side as in steps *5* and *6*.

⑦

⑧

Pocket

Insertion

Insertion

Pocket

(×6)

Open Frame I—Bow-tie Motif

Although the centers of the individual sides tend to bulge upward in large solid figures made this way, the finishing is clean and strong and the final forms are beautiful and reflect the true nature of origami. I especially like the bow-tie motif appearing on the surfaces.

Using the forms shown in "Polyhedrons Summarized" on p. 238, devise your own variations.

Open tower, 12-unit assembly

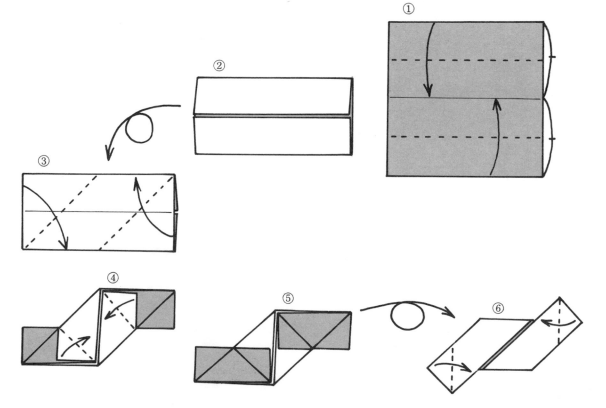

Assemblies of 30 (left) and 22 (right) units

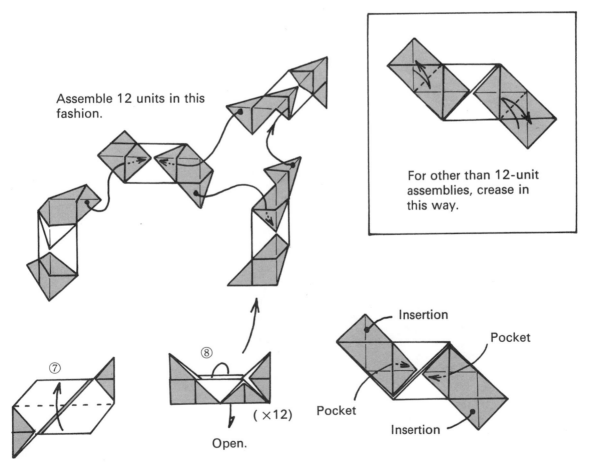

Assemble 12 units in this fashion.

For other than 12-unit assemblies, crease in this way.

⑦

⑧

(×12)

Open.

Insertion

Pocket

Pocket

Insertion

Assembly of 48 units (left) and 2 12-unit assemblies connected (right)

Assembly of 60 units

Open Frame II
—Plain

Although it is not as colorful as open frame I with the bow-tie motif, this revised unit manifests no bulging of individual sides. Consequently it is more versatile and can be assembled in a surprising number of ways.

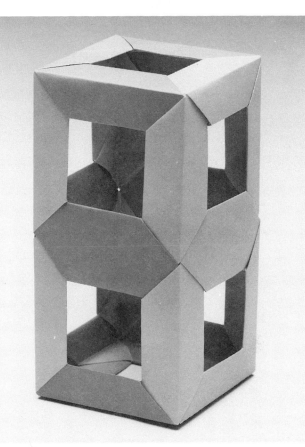

Open frame II, 20-unit assembly

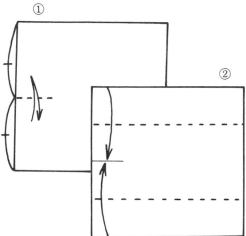

① ②

③

④

Make a crease.

⑤

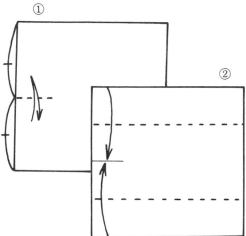

⑥

Insert and fold.

⑦

⑧

Continued on next page.

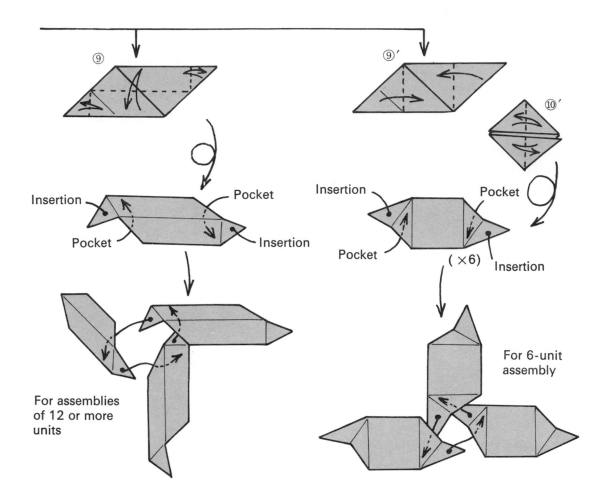

⑨

⑨′

⑩′

Insertion   Pocket

Pocket   Insertion

Insertion   Pocket

Pocket   Insertion

(×6)

For assemblies
of 12 or more
units

For 6-unit
assembly

Two-story tower with a pitched roof, 25-unit assembly (left); assemblies of 28 (middle)
and 20 (right) units

Assemblies of 12 (left), 6 (middle), and 84 (right) units

Assembly of 28 units on p. 66, seen from a different angle

Multistory, towerlike structures with pitched roofs can be produced from open frame II in an almost architectural fashion. And creases can be added or not according to a predetermined architectural design.

Snub Cube with Windows

Before folding, cut a rectangular piece of paper 1 : $\sqrt{2}$ in half along the long axis. Refer to No. 17 in "Polyhedrons Summarized" on p. 239. Assemble these units to produce the solid with 6 rectangular forms attached as if in a twisted line.

Eight triangular windows and small windows in the six rectangular forms will result.

1 : $\sqrt{2}$

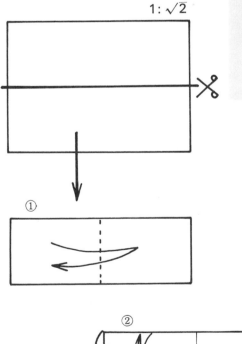

①

②

③

④

Open.

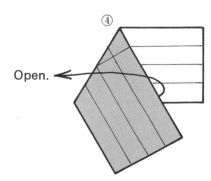

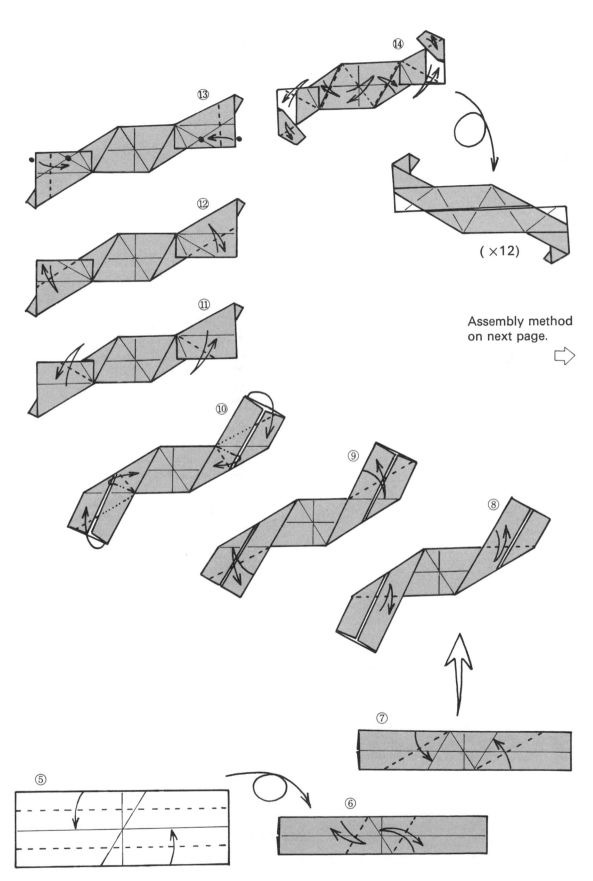

⑭

(×12)

⑬

Assembly method
on next page.
⇨

⑫

⑪

⑩

⑨

⑧

⑦

⑤

⑥

69

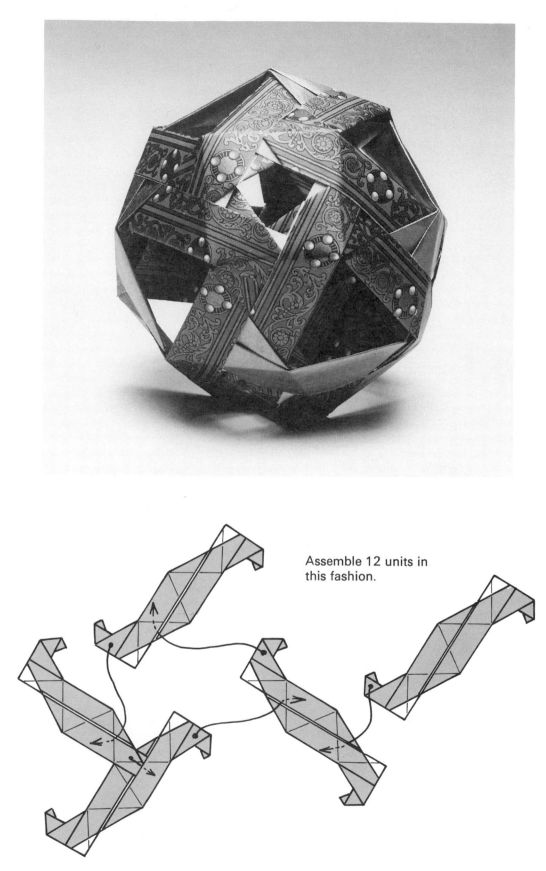

Assemble 12 units in
this fashion.

Chapter 3: Cubes Plus Alpha

In this chapter, various elements are added to cubes to see how they can change. The well-known Sonobè system is one of the methods employed.

Simple Sonobè 6-unit Assembly Plus Alpha (by Kunihiko Kasahara)

Inevitable Slits
Each surface of the simple Sonobè 6-unit assembly (as proposed by
Kunihiko Kasahara) is marked with an × made up of slits resulting inevi-
tably —without use of scissors or adhesive —from unit-origami folding.
Although they might seem useless or even undesirable, these slits actually
enable us to add many different elements to the Sonobè cube.

Cube (left) and cube with
pyramids added (right)

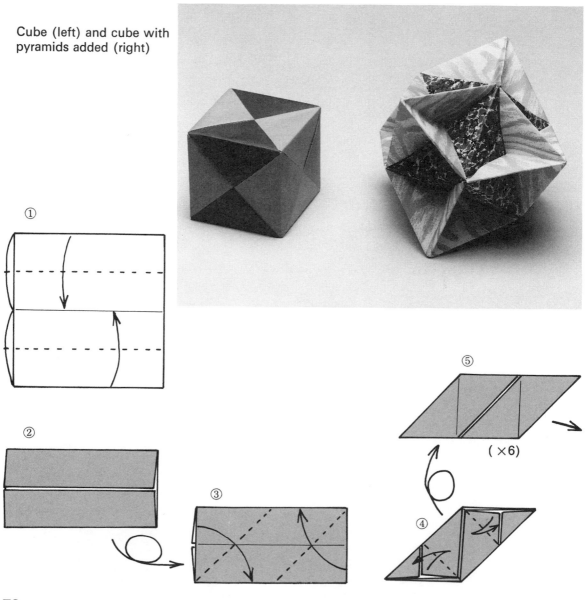

① ② ③ ④ ⑤

(×6)

Element No. 1   Pyramid

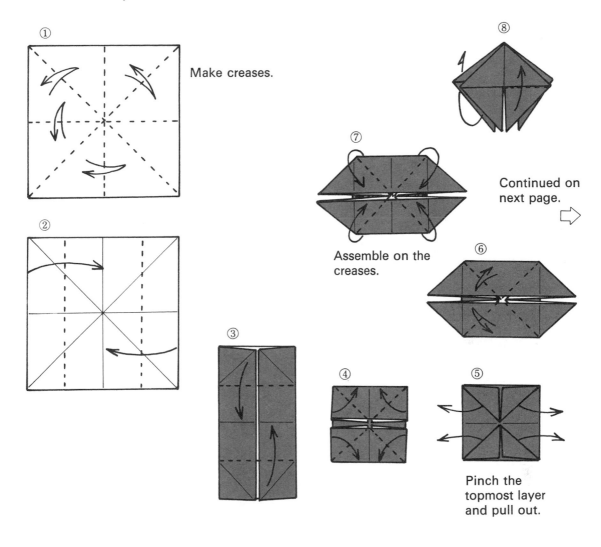

① Make creases.

②

③

④

⑤ Pinch the topmost layer and pull out.

⑥

⑦ Assemble on the creases.

⑧

Continued on next page. ⇨

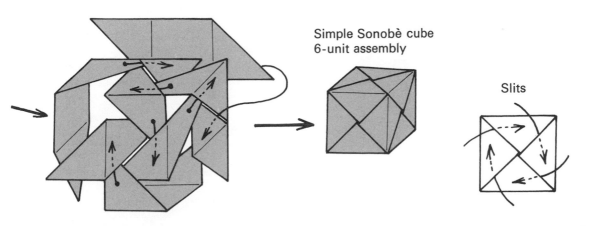

Simple Sonobè cube 6-unit assembly

Slits

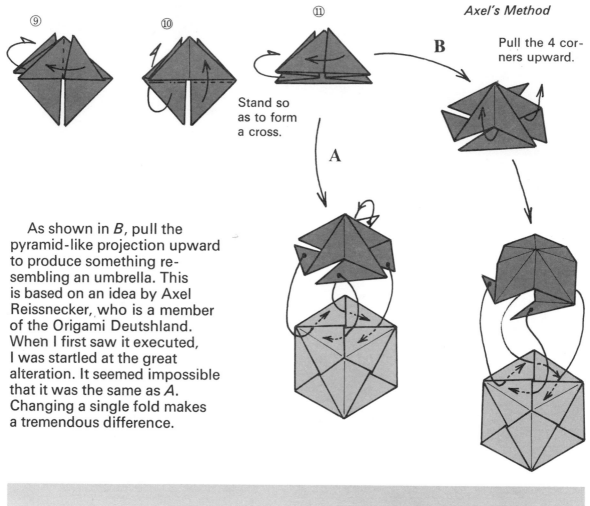

⑨ ⑩ ⑪

B Pull the 4 corners upward.

Stand so as to form a cross.

A

As shown in *B*, pull the pyramid-like projection upward to produce something resembling an umbrella. This is based on an idea by Axel Reissnecker, who is a member of the Origami Deutshland. When I first saw it executed, I was startled at the great alteration. It seemed impossible that it was the same as *A*. Changing a single fold makes a tremendous difference.

A method (left) and Axel's *B* method (right)

Element No. 2
Two-tone Pyramid

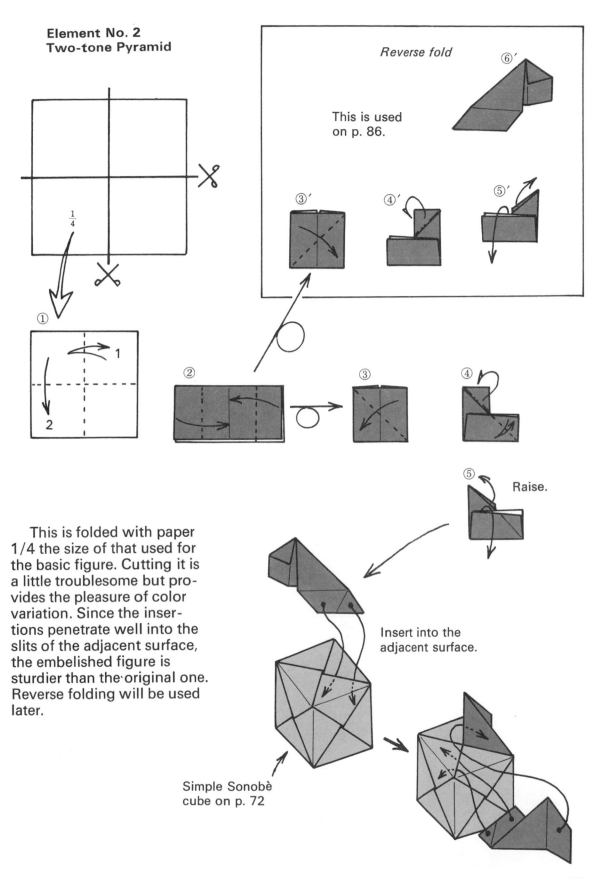

$\frac{1}{4}$

① 1 2

② ③ ④

⑤ Raise.

Reverse fold

This is used on p. 86.

⑥′

③′ ④′ ⑤′

Insert into the adjacent surface.

This is folded with paper 1/4 the size of that used for the basic figure. Cutting it is a little troublesome but provides the pleasure of color variation. Since the insertions penetrate well into the slits of the adjacent surface, the embelished figure is sturdier than the original one. Reverse folding will be used later.

Simple Sonobè cube on p. 72

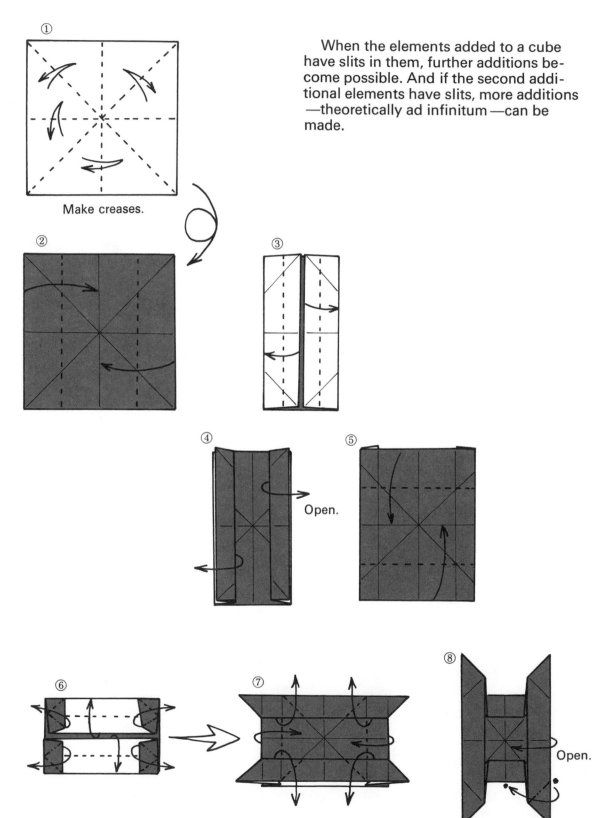

① Make creases.

When the elements added to a cube have slits in them, further additions become possible. And if the second additional elements have slits, more additions —theoretically ad infinitum —can be made.

②

③

④ Open.

⑤

⑥

⑦

⑧ Open.

⑯

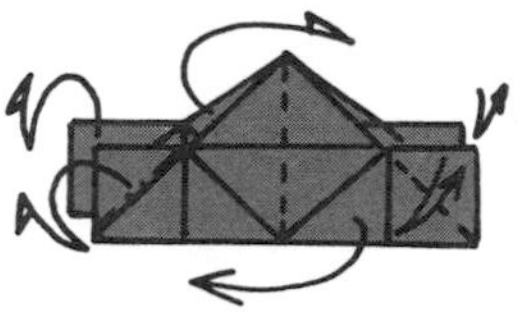

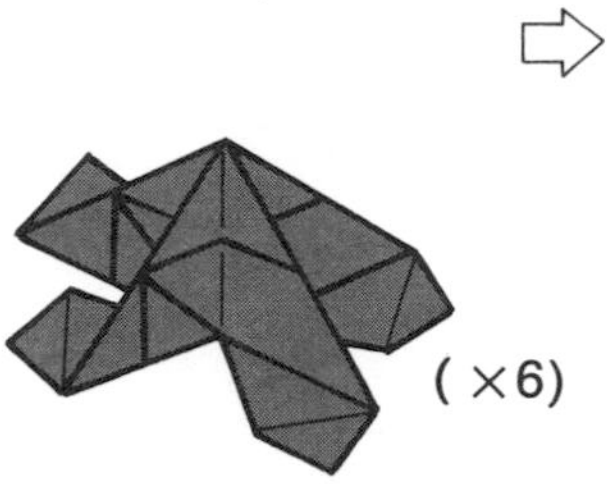

After creasing,
open into a cross.

Assembly method
on p. 79.

(×6)

⑮

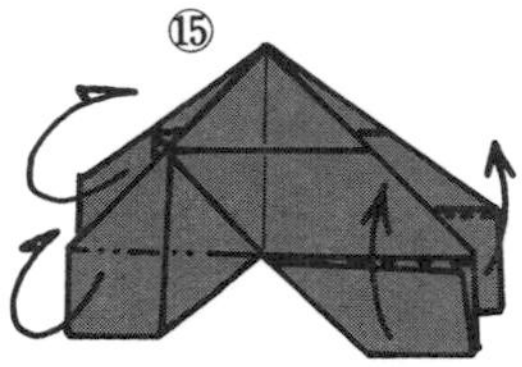

⑭

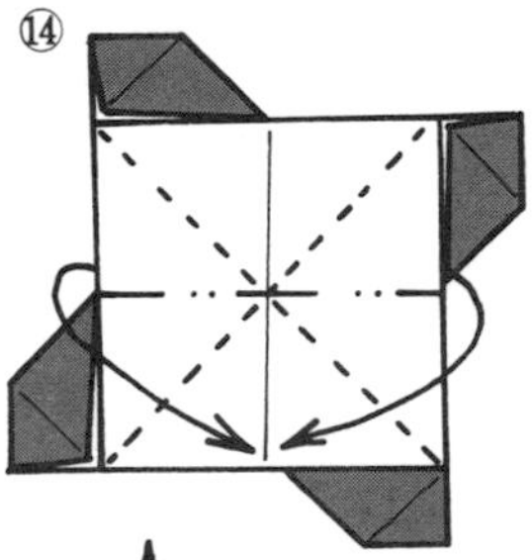

Fold and assem-
ble on creases.

⑬

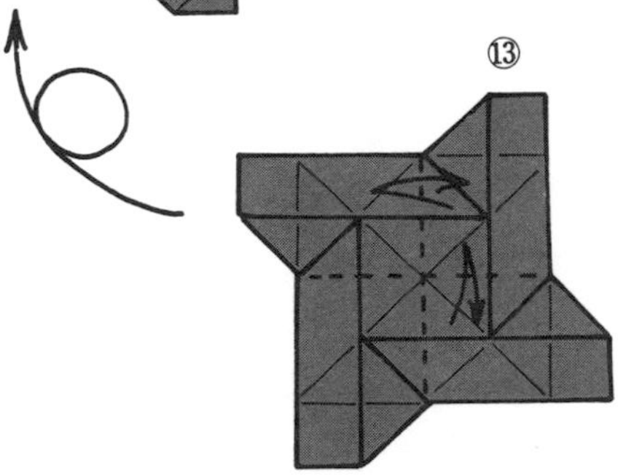

Fold the 3 points as
in steps 8–11.

⑫

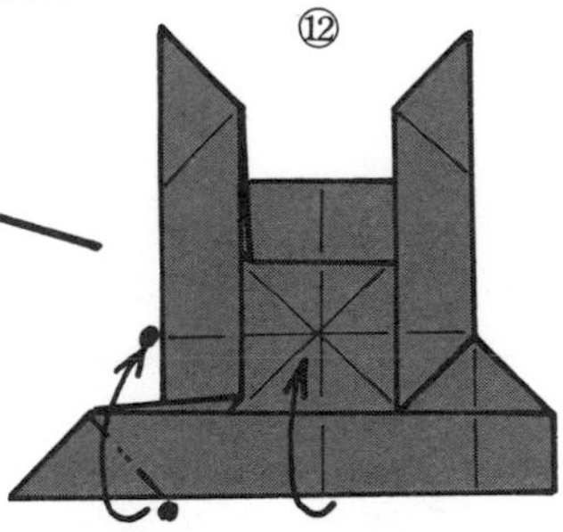

⑨

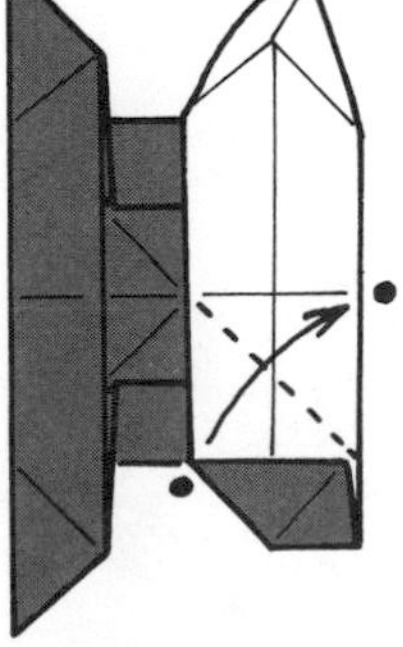

⑩

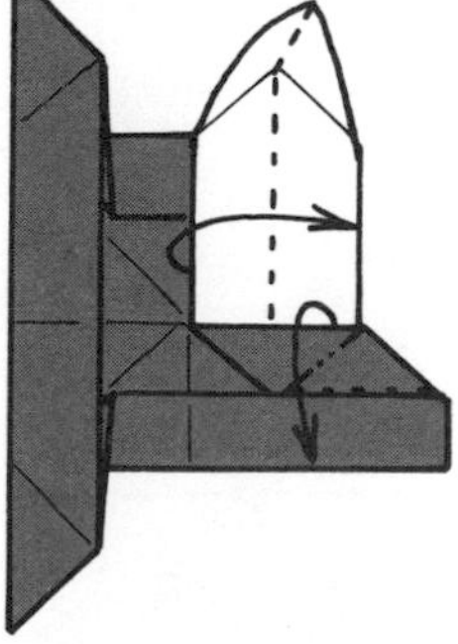

⑪

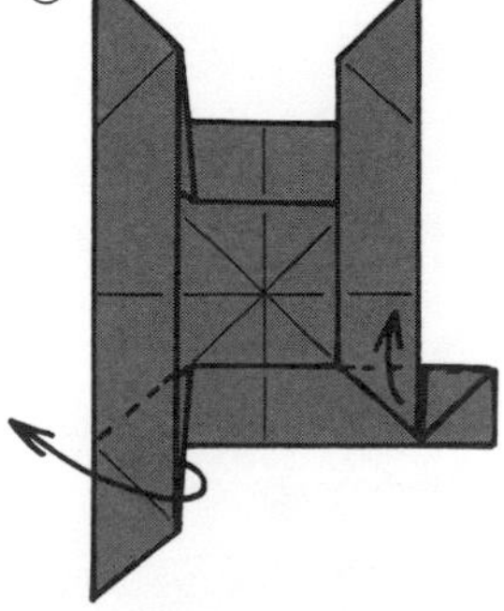

77

Element No. 4

For the second set of additions, the paper is about 1/16 the size of that used in the basic figure; and the finished element is fairly small. Although it is less splendid than the amount of work it requires might seem to warrant, I include this figure because its form is rhythmical and pleasing. In the case of the large elements, insert points into the adjacent surface, as on p. 75. You should be able to devise further small elements on your own.

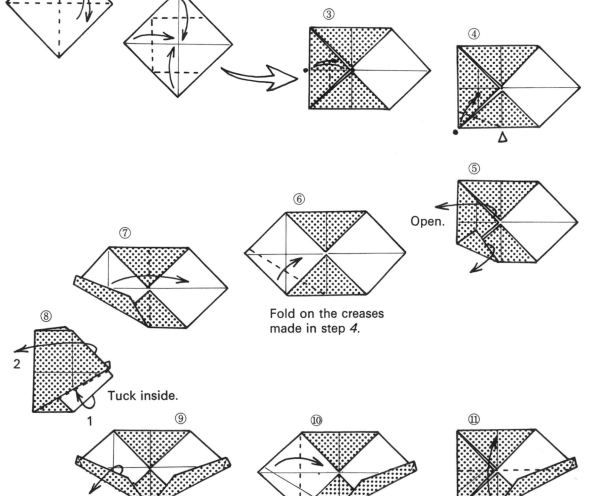

$\frac{1}{16}$

③

④

⑤ Open.

⑥

Fold on the creases made in step *4*.

⑦

⑧

2

Tuck inside.

1

⑨

⑩

⑪

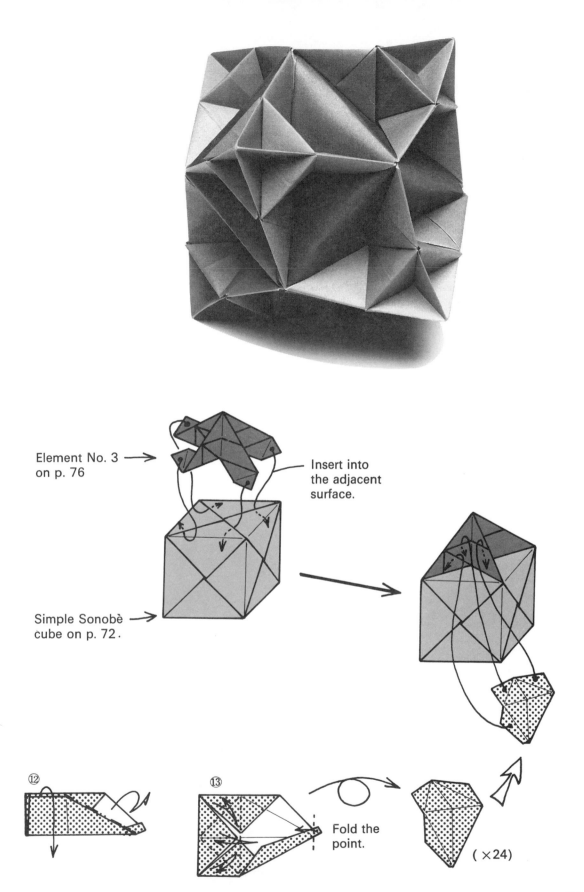

Element No. 3
on p. 76

Insert into
the adjacent
surface.

Simple Sonobè
cube on p. 72.

⑫

⑬

Fold the
point.

(×24)

Simple Sonobè 12-unit Assembly Plus Alpha

In this larger cube, the slits on the faces form plus marks instead of × marks. As is shown below, there are 2 equally good methods of assembling this cube (A and B). Once it is made, we can proceed to the elements that are to be added to it.

The pyramid employed with the 6-unit assembly can be used with the 12-unit assembly too if the points are folded in reverse. Either the 2-tone element or the element with slits will work. This is both extremely convenient and highly interesting. There are slits on the edges of the 12-unit assembly into which additional Elements No. 2 can be inserted.

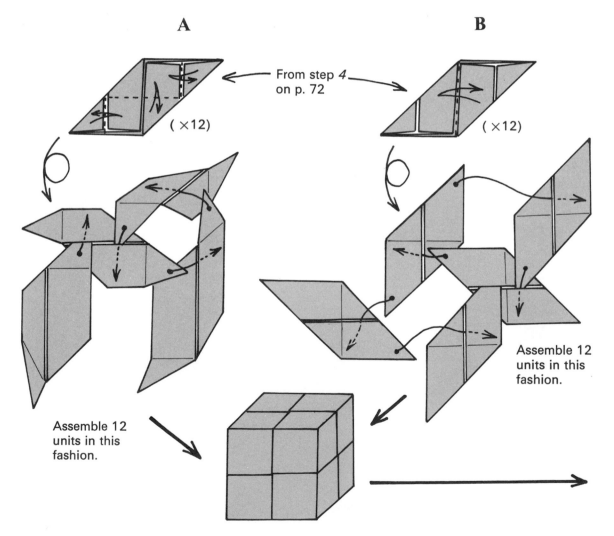

A

B

From step *4* on p. 72

(×12)

(×12)

Assemble 12 units in this fashion.

Assemble 12 units in this fashion.

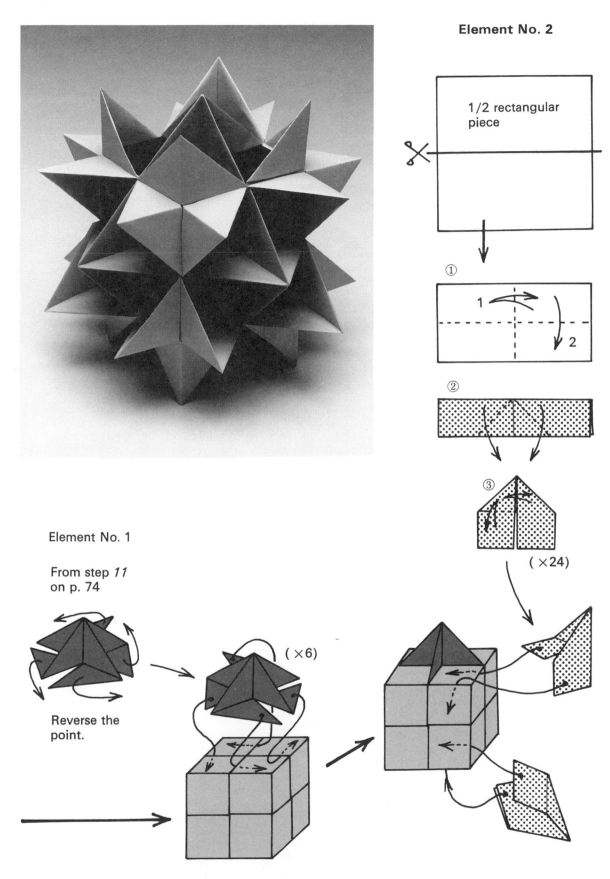

Element No. 2

1/2 rectangular piece

① 1 2

②

③

(×24)

Element No. 1

From step *11*
on p. 74

Reverse the
point.

(×6)

81

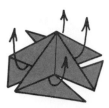

Pull 4 points upward.

(×6)

Cube with Elements No. 1 added according to Axel's method

In the case of this Element No. 2, as well, it is possible to use Axel Reissnecker's idea (p. 74) and to pull up and insert the 4 points of the pyramid.

The resulting form has an entirely different appearance. Amuse yourself by trying out various assemblies.

Cube with Elements No. 1 added according to Axel's method and with Elements No. 2

82

Element No. 3

Another pyramid element. The joints are concealed underneath. When they are inserted, the pyramid covers half the surface of the cube.

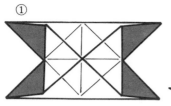

①

From step *9*
on p. 58

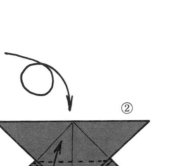

②

③

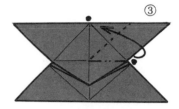

④

⑤

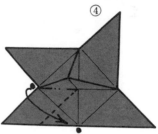

⑥

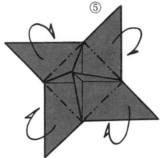

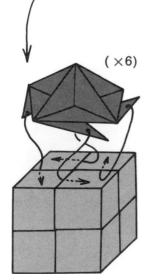

(×6)

12-unit assembly
on p. 80

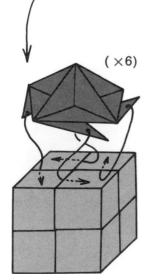

83

Double-pocket Unit

This extremely convenient unit has 2 pockets for insertions. Although less apparent in the case of 6-unit assemblies (see photograph below), its advantages become much more interesting in 12- or 24-unit assemblies.

Mixed upper- and under-side assembly (left) and under-side assembly (right)

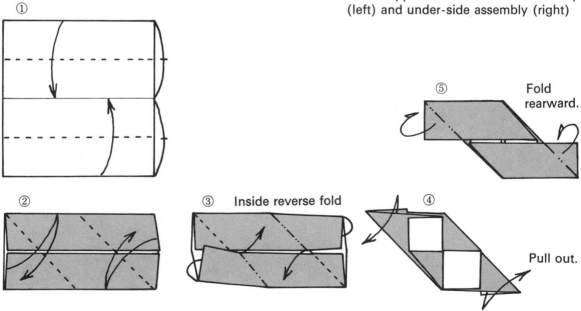

① ② ③ Inside reverse fold ④ Pull out. ⑤ Fold rearward.

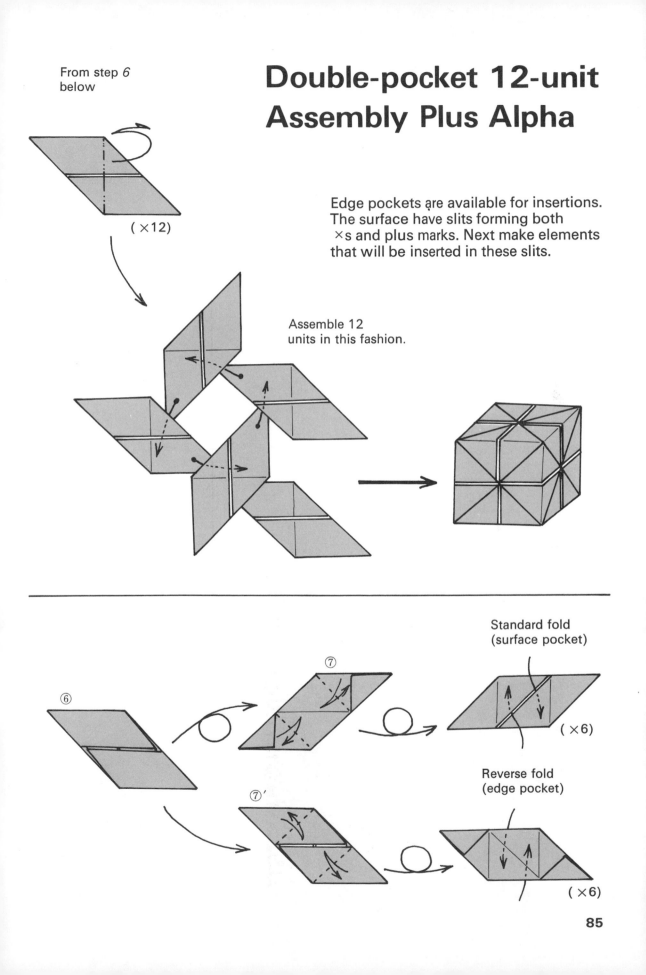

From step *6*
below

(×12)

Double-pocket 12-unit
Assembly Plus Alpha

Edge pockets are available for insertions.
The surface have slits forming both
×s and plus marks. Next make elements
that will be inserted in these slits.

Assemble 12
units in this fashion.

⑥

⑦

⑦′

Standard fold
(surface pocket)

(×6)

Reverse fold
(edge pocket)

(×6)

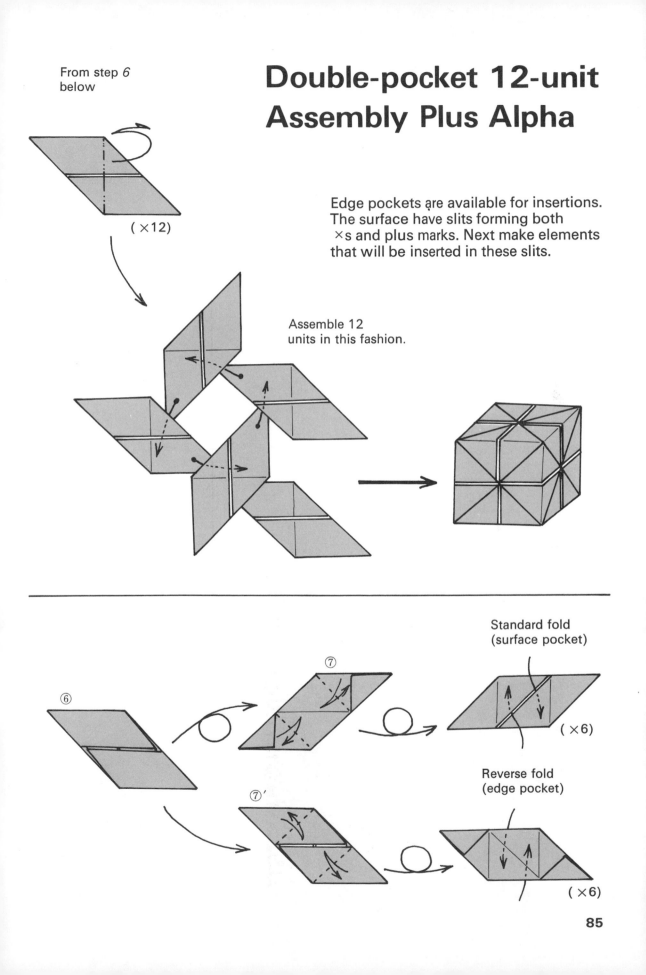

Element No. 1

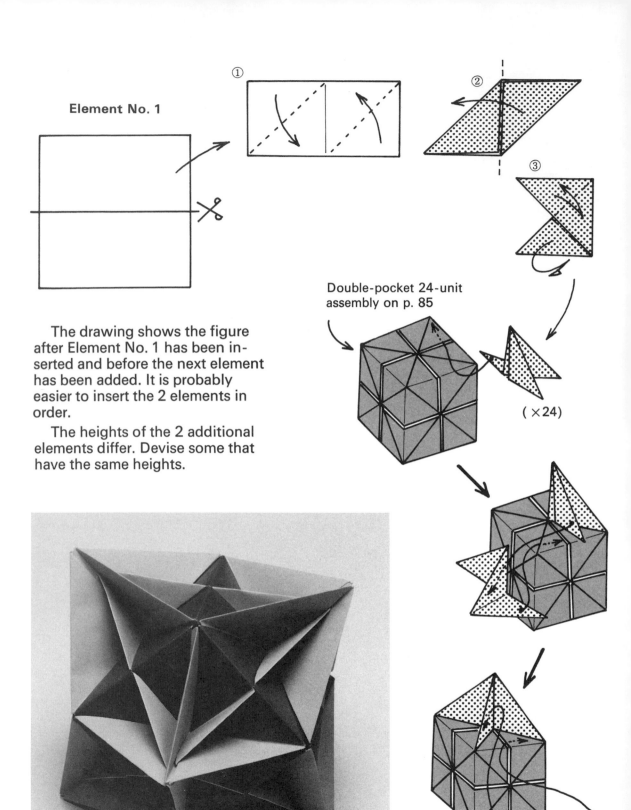

The drawing shows the figure after Element No. 1 has been inserted and before the next element has been added. It is probably easier to insert the 2 elements in order.

The heights of the 2 additional elements differ. Devise some that have the same heights.

Double-pocket 24-unit assembly on p. 85

(×24)

Reverse of fold on p. 75

(×24)

Double-pocket 24-unit Assembly Plus Alpha

The unit may be folded according to instructions on p. 84, but the finished work is neater and has fewer exposed creases if folded as shown in steps *1–5*. Since the units are inserted in slits in the edges, the foldings must be the reverse of that shown on p. 85.

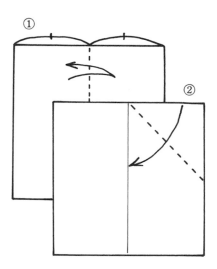

① ②

③

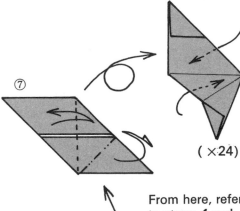

⑦

(×24)

From here, refer to steps *4* and following on p. 84.

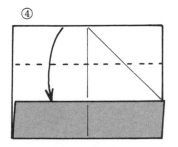

④

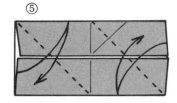

⑤

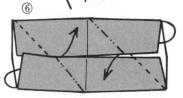

⑥

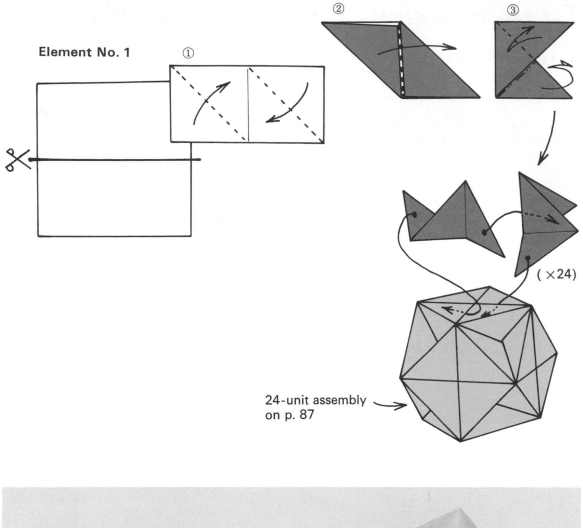

Element No. 1

① ② ③

(×24)

24-unit assembly
on p. 87

Solid figure composed of a 24-unit (edge-slit) reverse assembly (left) and a similar solid with additional elements appended (right)

Element No. 2

This element is to be added to the triangular concavity in the 24-unit assembly. The paper should be 1/4 as large as that used in making the basic figure. It might be interesting to make this element more sharply pointed if it is to be added together with the Element No. 1 (p. 88).

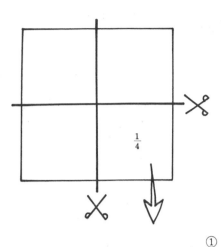

$\frac{1}{4}$

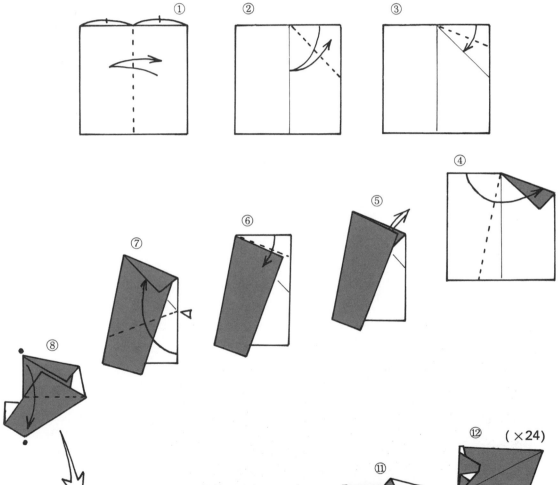

① ② ③ ④ ⑤ ⑥ ⑦ ⑧ ⑨ ⑩ ⑪

Stand.

⑫ (×24)

Assembly method on next page.

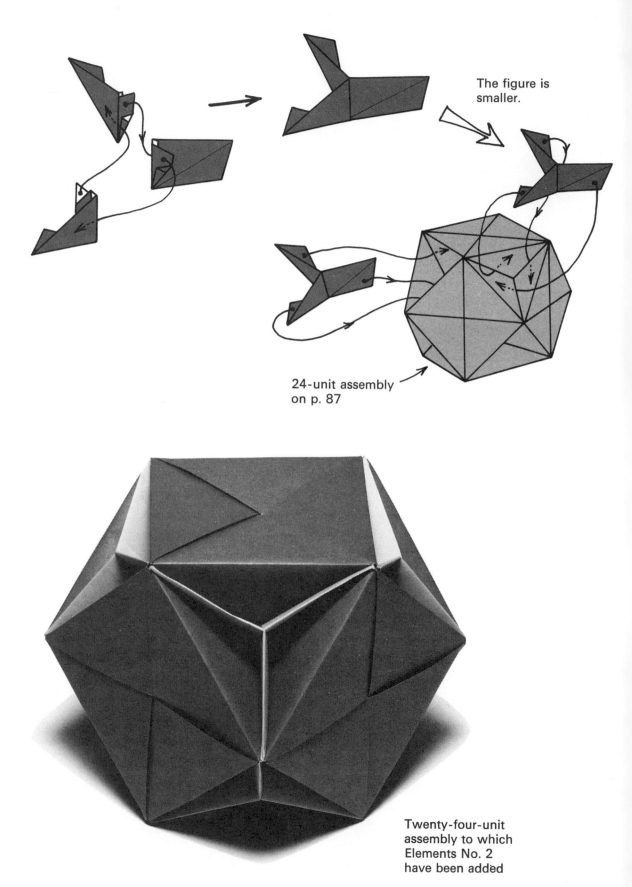

The figure is smaller.

24-unit assembly
on p. 87

Twenty-four-unit
assembly to which
Elements No. 2
have been added

Variations on the Double-pocket Unit

With slight changes in folds it is possible to produce brilliant solid figures with variations of double-pocket units. The moment I saw the "Star Decorative Ball" by Hachiro Kamata, I felt certain it could be made with double-pocket units. I then produced F on p. 95. There would be no point in assembling F as a cube.

Assembly of 6 units

A

① From step *4* on p. 84

②

③ Fold the other side in the same way.

④

⑤

⑦

⑧ **A**

Pull out.

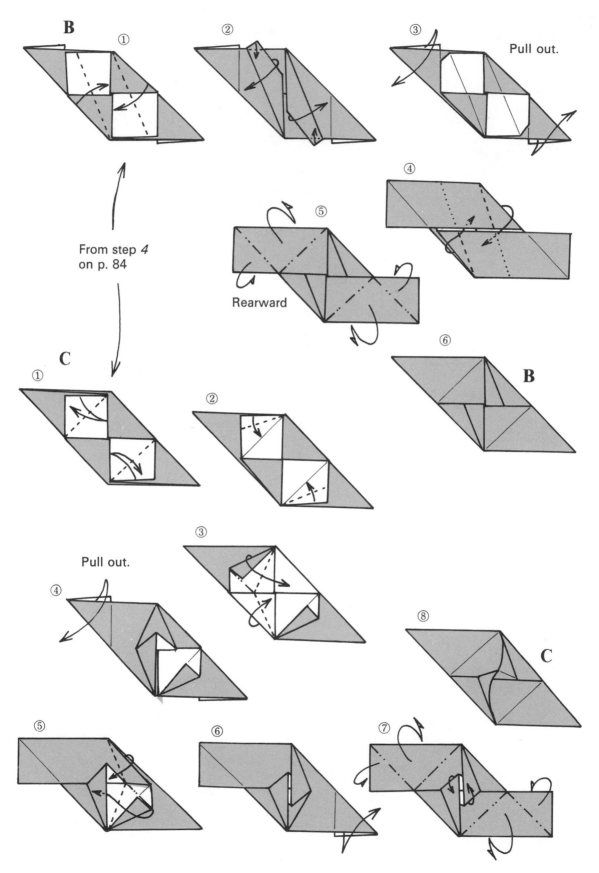

B

① ② ③ Pull out.

④

⑤

Rearward

⑥

B

From step *4* on p. 84

C

① ②

③

Pull out.

④

⑧

C

⑤ ⑥ ⑦

D

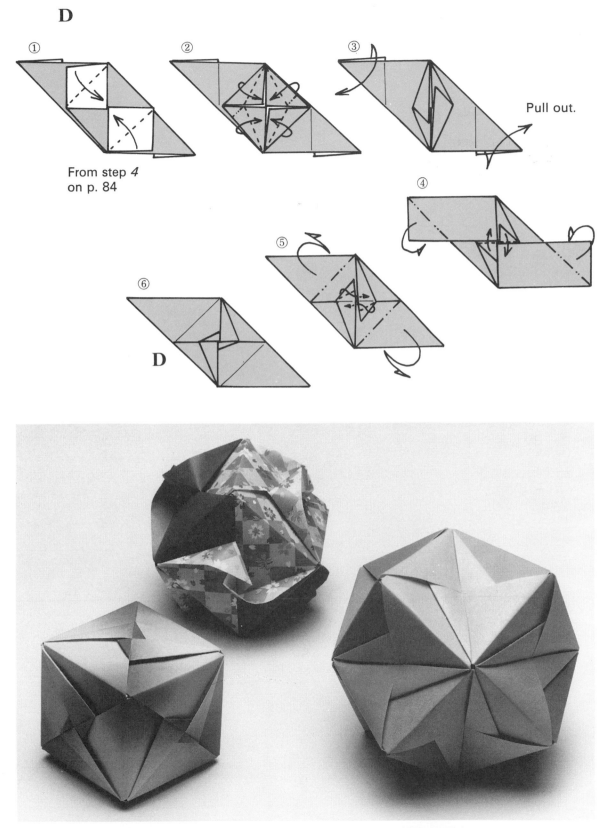

① From step *4* on p. 84

② ③ Pull out.

④

⑤

⑥ D

Assemblies of 6 *D* (left), 6 *C* (middle), and 12 *B* (right)

E

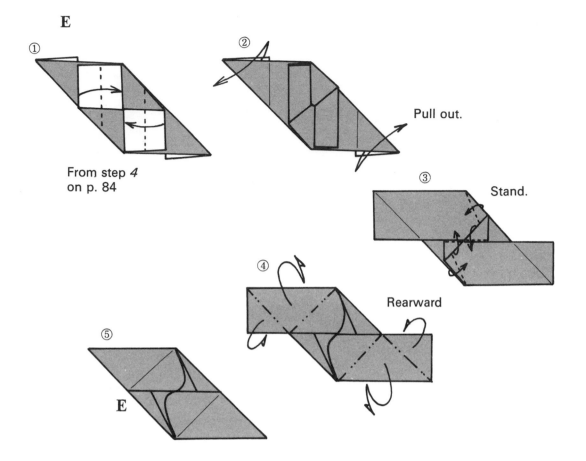

① From step *4* on p. 84

② Pull out.

③ Stand.

④ Rearward

⑤ **E**

Assemblies of 12 *E* (left) and 6 *E* (right)

F

① Pull out.

②

③ Rearward

From step *4*
on p. 84.

④

⑤ As you open,
fold in half.

Assembly of 30 *F*

⑥

Inside reverse fold

⑦

⑧ Open.

⑨ **F**

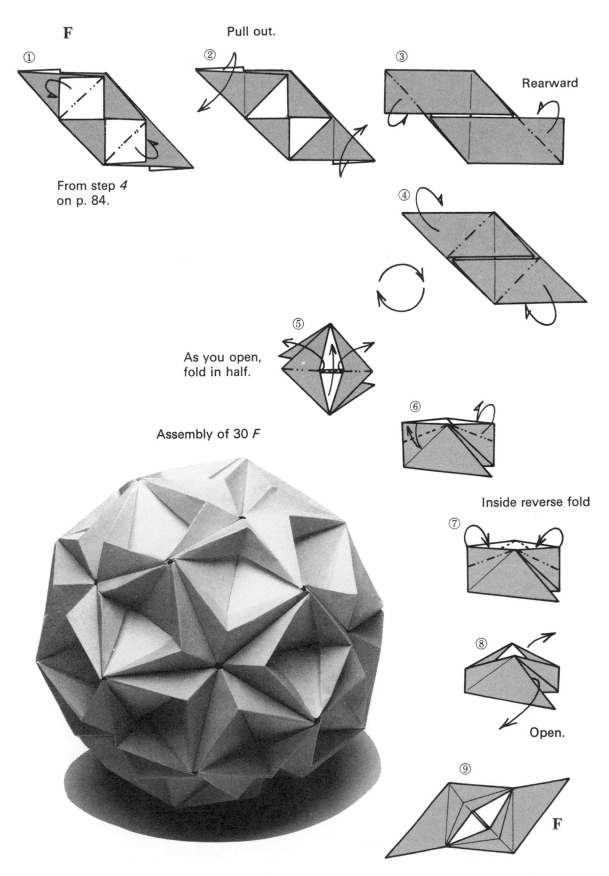

Square Units—Square Windows

The assembly method for this square unit with square windows is shown on the next page. Because of the hooking assembly, the last few units are hard to work with, but the finished figure is strong and firm.

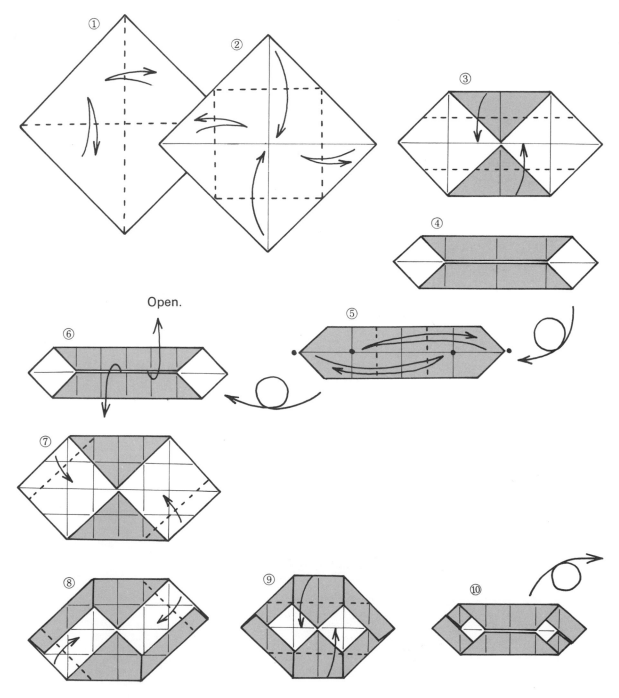

Open.

96

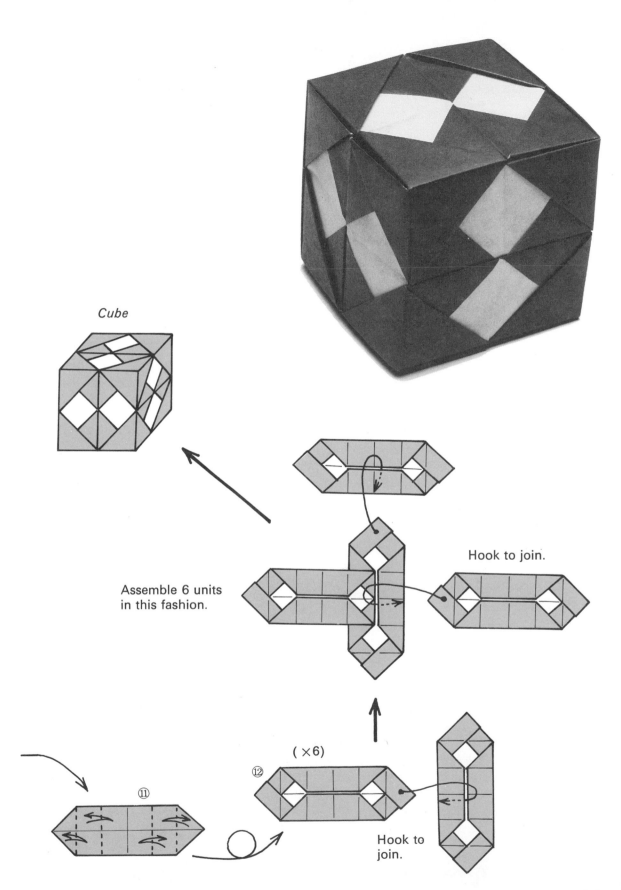

Cube

Assemble 6 units
in this fashion.

Hook to join.

Hook to join.

(×6)

⑪

⑫

Hook to
join.

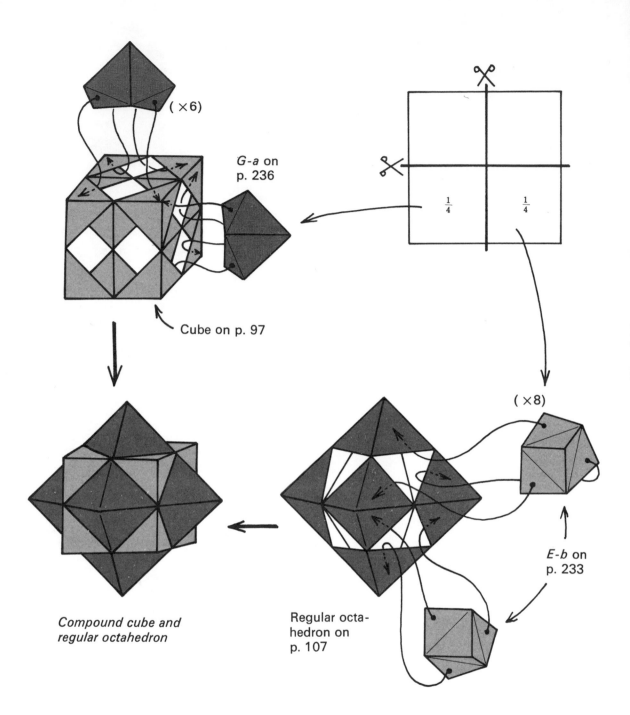

(×6)

G-a on
p. 236

Cube on p. 97

¼   ¼

(×8)

E-b on
p. 233

Regular octa-
hedron on
p. 107

*Compound cube and
regular octahedron*

As shown in the drawings, square windows appear in the surfaces of the cube. These are filled with quadrangular elements made of 2 *G-a* on p. 236. The similar unit made of 1 sheet (p. 233) may be used, although it is structurally weaker.

Interestingly, adding elements to this cube and adding elements to the regular octahedron on p. 107 produce precisely the same final form.

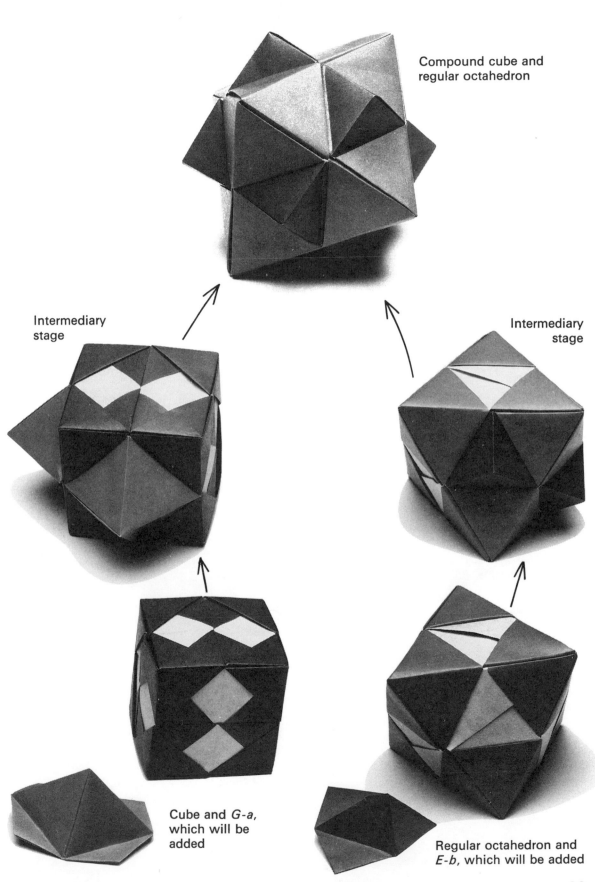

Compound cube and
regular octahedron

Intermediary
stage

Intermediary
stage

Cube and *G-a*,
which will be
added

Regular octahedron and
E-b, which will be added

99

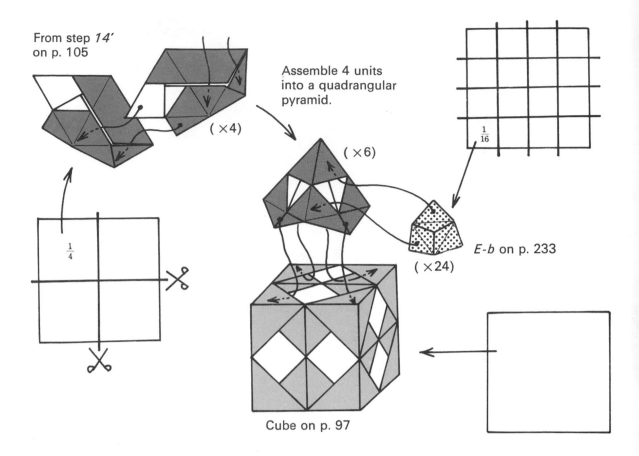

From step *14′* on p. 105

(×4)

Assemble 4 units into a quadrangular pyramid.

(×6)

$\frac{1}{16}$

$\frac{1}{4}$

E-b on p. 233

(×24)

Cube on p. 97

In the figure in the drawing on the preceding page, first the unit in step *14'* on p. 105 has been added to the square windows of the cube on p. 97. Since the small units are made of paper 1/4 and 1/16 the size of that of the basic unit, start with a large piece (10 inches or 25 centimeters to a side). This unit may be added to figures other than the cube (see photograph below). The square windows may be filled with other units as shown in the photograph on the preceding page. Try your hand at devising further interesting assembly methods.

On the left is a 10-unit assembly plus *G-a*; on the right a 30-unit assembly plus *G-a*.

Strength from Weakness: A Big Advantage of Unit Origami

Solid figures made by assembling units without adhesive are weak and lack sharpness of definition. But working with insertions and slits showed me that the slits forming naturally on surfaces and edges of unit origami are actually an advantage opening up a whole new world of delight and compensating for structural weakness and lack of sharpness.

The Charm of Changing a Single Crease

A slight change of no more than a single crease —as I said in talking about the open frame —can open whole new horizons. It is as if we had been playing in a front yard and suddenly discovered the key to a door leading to a wonderful, heretofore unknown inner garden. To be able to determine the limitations of a unit once and for all would be convenient. But in my case, I frequently look at an old origami and suddenly discover new ways of using old units. This is a source of both surprise and delight.

The wonder of the new worlds that emerge from altering single folds is not limited to unit origami but can be seen in origami animal folds as well. For instance; a single fold's difference in a beak turns an origami crow into a small bird or into a parrot. Taking free advantage of this ability to work changes enables us to produce highly realistic origami. Changing a single crease in unit origami opens new worlds; doing the same thing in animal origami leads to an entirely different world.

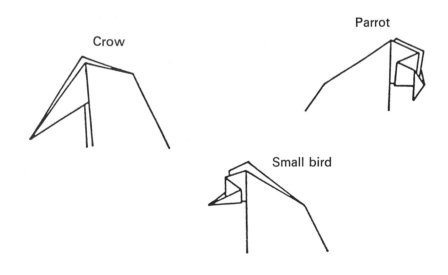

Crow

Parrot

Small bird

Chapter 4: The Equilateral Triangle Plus Alpha

In this chapter we shall be adding elements to solid figures with equilateral-triangular faces. Replacing flat surfaces with projections and recessions generates many different kinds of beauty.

Equilateral Triangles—Triangular Windows

Combining 2 of the same element to make a single unit. A variation in folding lines (shown in the box on the next page) was used in the work on p. 100. The unit is a brother to the square windows on p. 96.

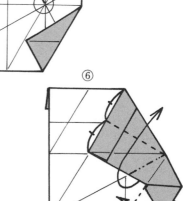

Standard fold

From step *6* of *B* on p. 231

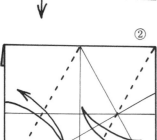

⑤ Fold to ○ mark.

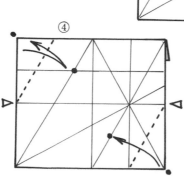

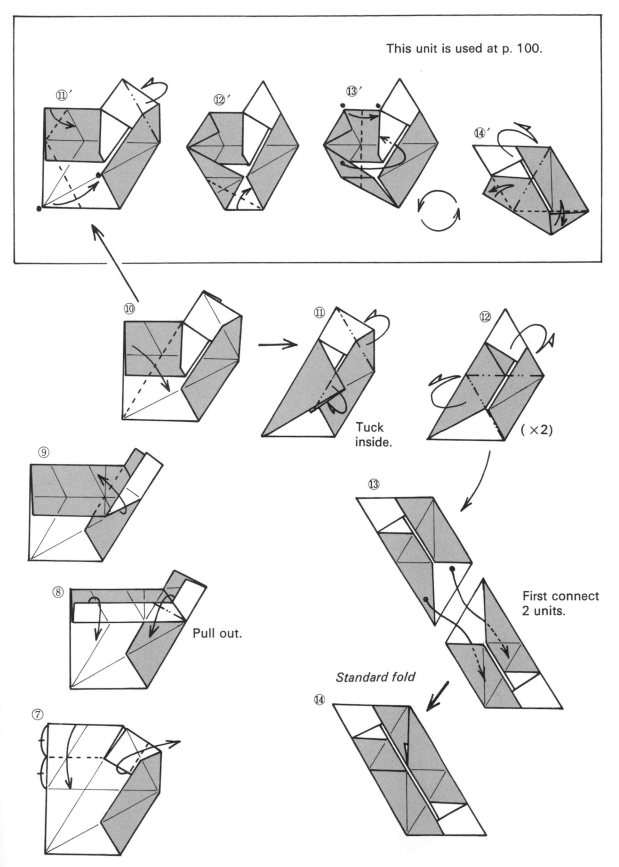

This unit is used at p. 100.

⑪′ ⑫′ ⑬′ ⑭′

⑩ ⑪ Tuck inside. ⑫ (×2)

⑨

⑧ Pull out.

⑬ First connect 2 units.

Standard fold

⑭

⑦

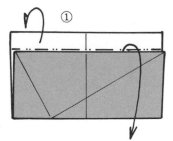

Reverse fold

From the reverse fold
of *B* on p. 231

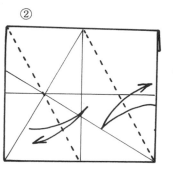

Employing the standard or the reverse
folding method (producing a mirror image
of the standard form) makes possible a
regular octahedron. This reverse fold is also
needed in making a regular tetrahedron or
a regular icosahedron.

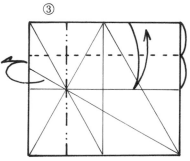

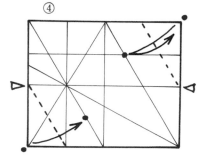

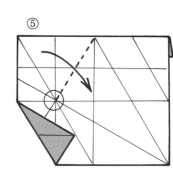

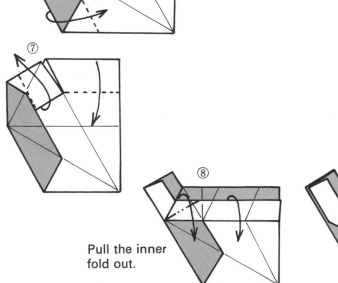

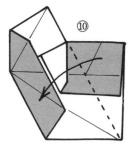

Pull the inner
fold out.

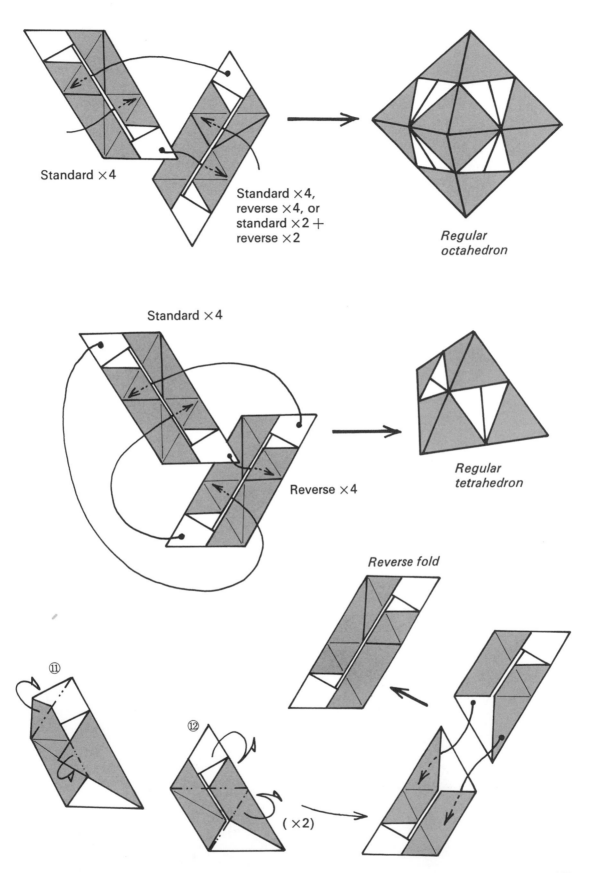

Standard ×4

Standard ×4,
reverse ×4, or
standard ×2 +
reverse ×2

*Regular
octahedron*

Standard ×4

Reverse ×4

*Regular
tetrahedron*

Reverse fold

⑪

⑫

(×2)

Triangular white blanks caused by the exposure of the underside of the paper characterize solid figures made with this unit.

Their interest is greatly increased by the possibility of inserting additional elements into the slits around those blanks.

The additional element is enclosed in the unit. Assembling a regular tetrahedron or icosahedron is easier and produces more beautiful results.

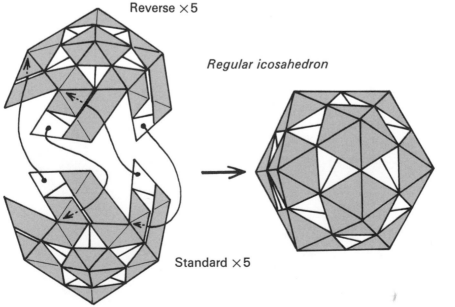

$\frac{1}{4}$ $\frac{1}{4}$

Regular tetrahedron

E-b on p. 233

F-b on p. 234 or *G-b* on p. 236

Regular octahedron

Reverse ×5

Regular icosahedron

Standard ×5

On the left is an 8-unit assembly plus *E-b*; on the right, a 20-unit assembly plus *E-b*

On the left is a 4-unit assembly plus *G-b* (or *F-b*); on the right, a 20-unit assembly plus *G-b* (or *F-b*).

Propeller Units

Although the folding order is slightly complicated, these units are interesting because alterations result in 4 different assembly methods. The completed solid figure is beautiful in itself, and decorating it with additional elements is very entertaining. In Japanese, these units are called *tomoè* because of an imagined resemblance to a pattern made up of three comma (*tomoè*) forms.

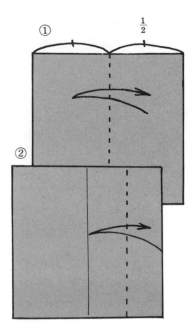

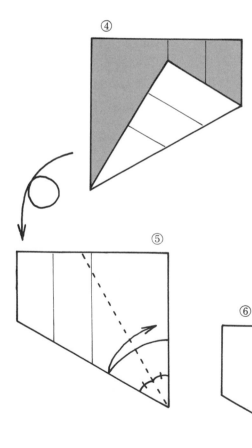

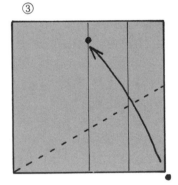

⑭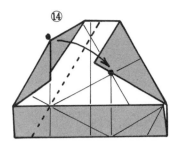

⑮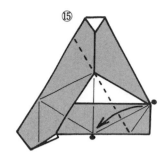

Continued on next page.

⑬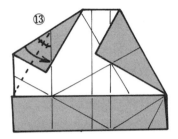

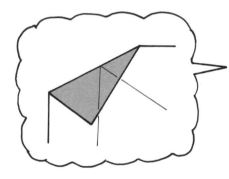 ⑫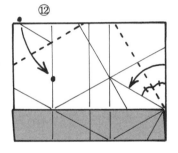

⑪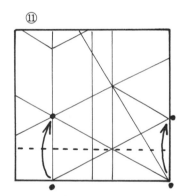

After creasing,
open completely.

⑧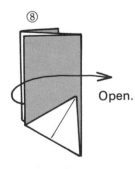

Open.

⑨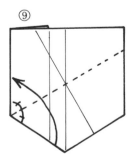

⑩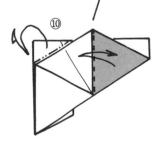

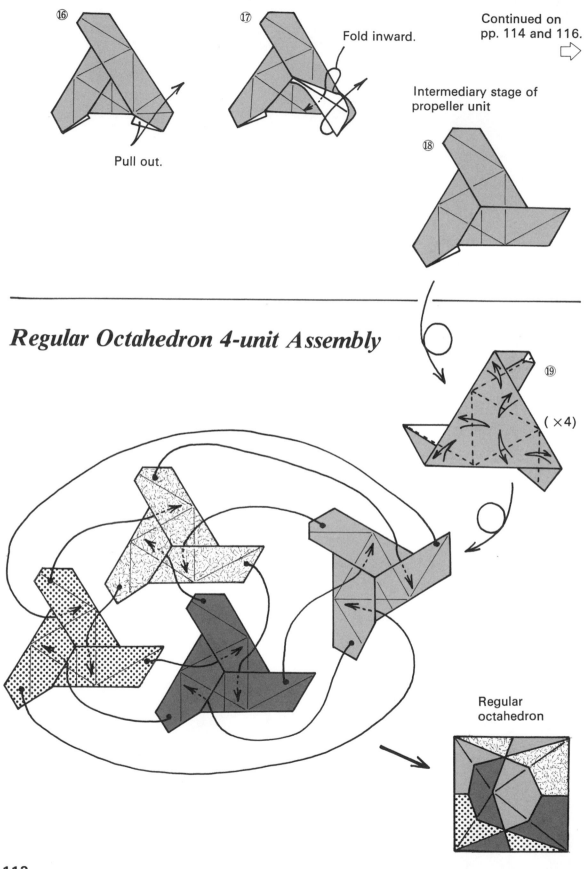

⑯

Pull out.

⑰ Fold inward.

Continued on pp. 114 and 116.

Intermediary stage of propeller unit

⑱

Regular Octahedron 4-unit Assembly

⑲

(×4)

Regular octahedron

Assemblies of the intermediary stage of propeller unit (step *19* on the preceding page): 8 unit (regular octahedron; left), 7 unit (middle), and 4 unit (right)

Step *17* represents a stage on the way to completion of the propeller unit. Because of overlappings, 2 of the 3 insertions become stiff and heavy. But this presents no problem, and results will be surprisingly sharp if the folding is clean and correct.

As shown on the preceding page, 4 of these units make a regular octahedron. This assembly method is better because more economical for using the same 4 units to create the same solid figure than the succeeding assembly methods. One of the solid figures shown in the photograph above is a regular octahedron made with the propeller unit on p. 116. This is an 8-unit assembly requiring paper twice as large as that used in the 4-unit assembly.

Regular Icosahedron 12-unit Assembly

From step *17*
on p. 112

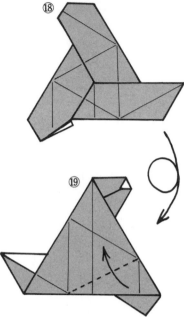

As long as you understand what you are doing thoroughly, do not worry if the 2-unit larger groups become shaky and wobbly during the assembly process.

It is possible to fold this with a single unit structured as shown in step *23*. Work out a way to do it for yourself.

Make 6 of these 2-unit sets. The assembly method is shown on the next page.

Assemble 2 of these units.

(×12)

(×6)

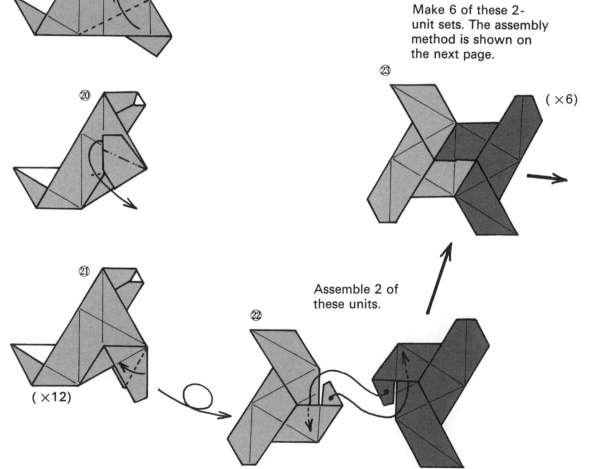

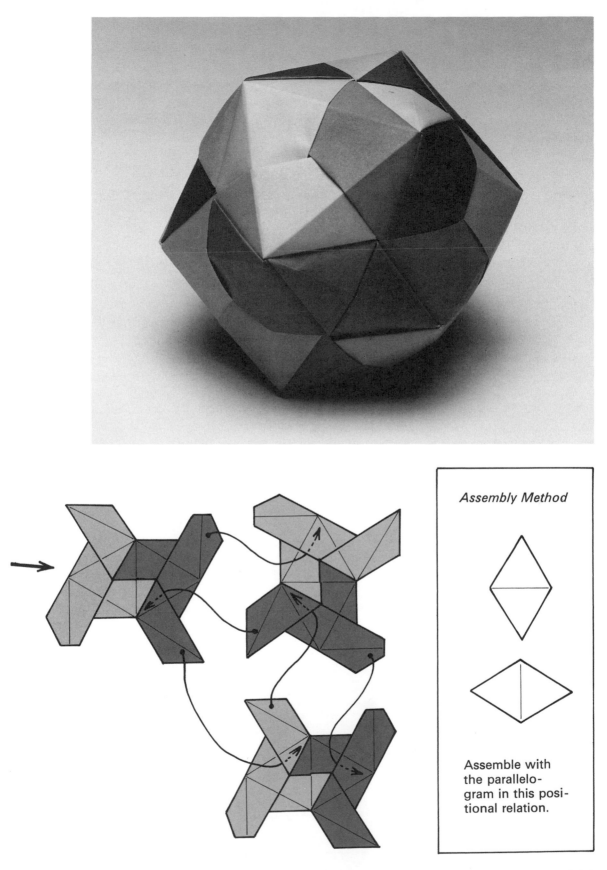

Assembly Method

Assemble with the parallelo-gram in this positional relation.

Completed Propeller Unit

Invert step *17*
on p. 112.

Any solid can be formed from it if the unit surfaces are equilateral triangles. Moreover, ordinary and inverted assemblies are possible. The inverted assembly is difficult to make and tends to fall apart, but completed solid figures made with it are surprisingly strong.

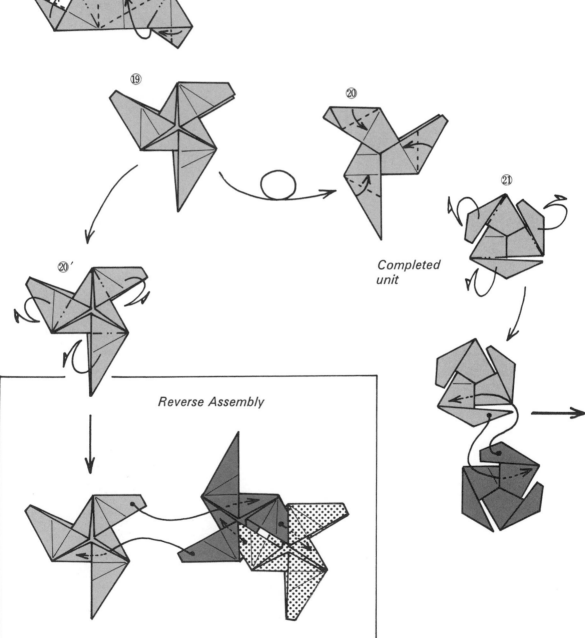

Completed
unit

Reverse Assembly

Regular icosahedron 20-unit assembly (left) and
regular tetrahedron 4-unit assembly (right)

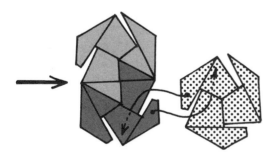

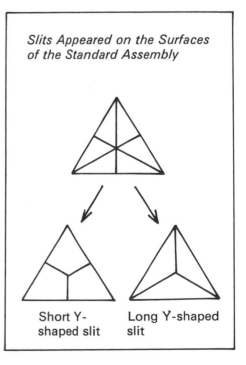

*Slits Appeared on the Surfaces
of the Standard Assembly*

Short Y-
shaped slit

Long Y-shaped
slit

Long Y-shaped and short Y-shaped
slits form on the surfaces of units assembled in the ordinary way (see drawing
on the right). Now we shall fold elements that
can be added to these units.

**Element No. 1 for the
Short-Y Form**

First make an element to insert in the
short Y-shaped slits. Varying colors for
the basic solid and the additional elements
produces many interesting effects.

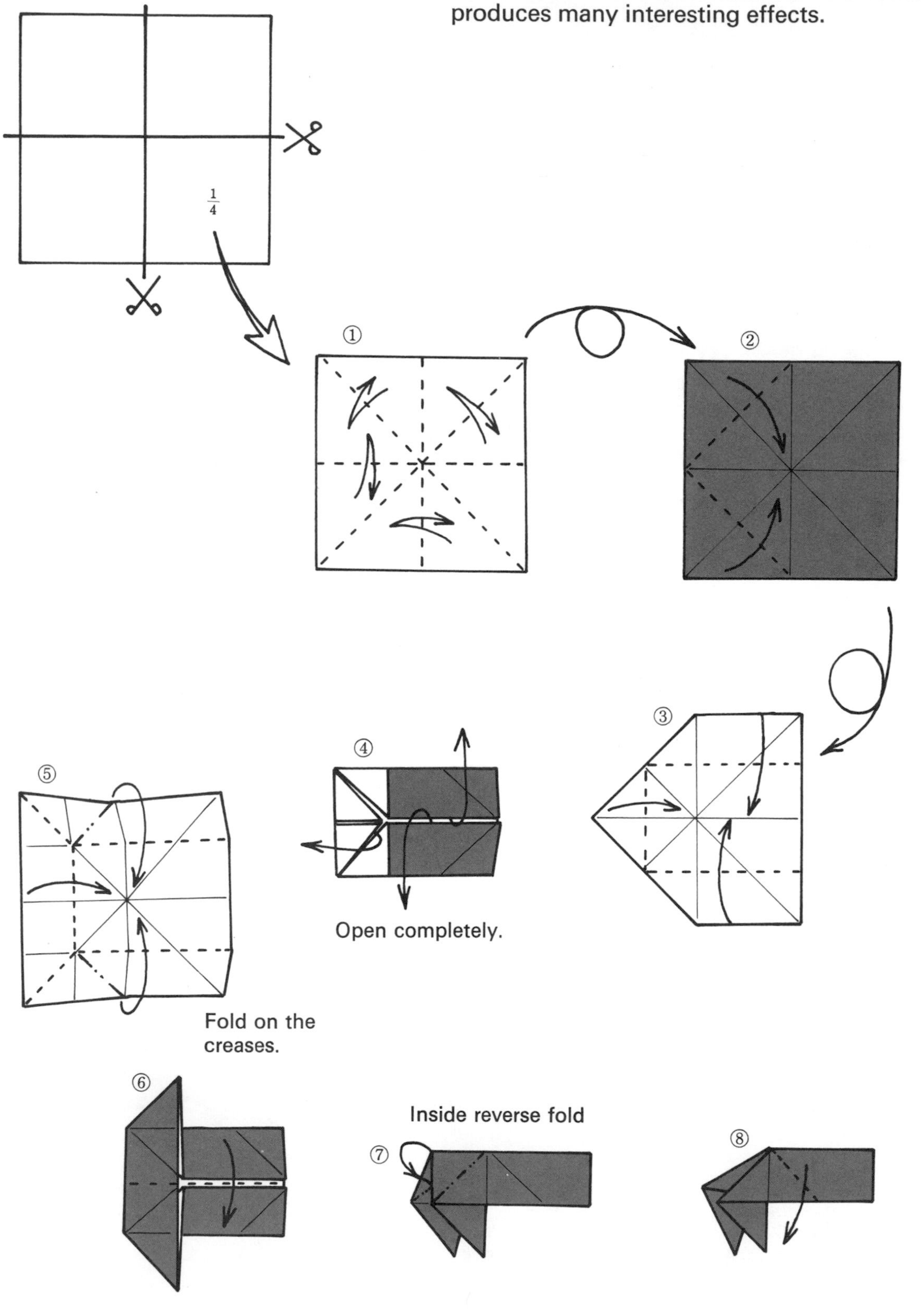

$\frac{1}{4}$

① ②

③

④

Open completely.

⑤

Fold on the
creases.

⑥

Inside reverse fold

⑦ ⑧

118

Regular tetrahedron 4-unit assembly
with Elements No. 1 added (left) and
regular icosahedxon 20-unit assembly
with Elements No. 1 added (right)

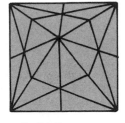

Solid figure as-
sembled with
propeller units
on p. 116

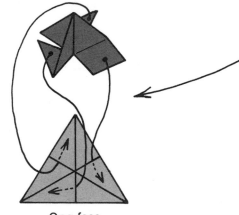

One face

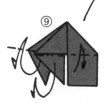

119

Element No. 2 for the Short-Y Form

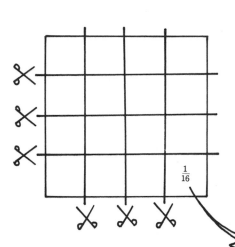

Used alone, this element provides pleasant color variation. Added to a basic solid in combinaiton with the long-Y-shaped element, it greatly enhances the beauty of the finished work. It is made from small paper only 1/16 the size of that used for the basic solid figure.

$\frac{1}{16}$

① $\frac{1}{4}$

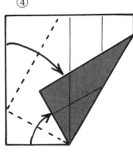

$\frac{1}{2}$

②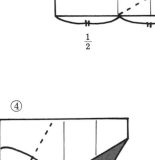

③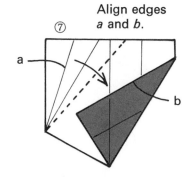

④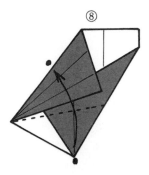

⑤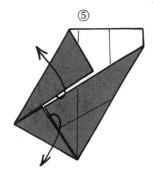

⑥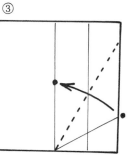

Align edges *a* and *b*.

⑦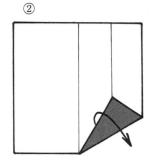

a

b

⑧

**Element No. 1 for
the Long-Y Form**

Continued on
next page.

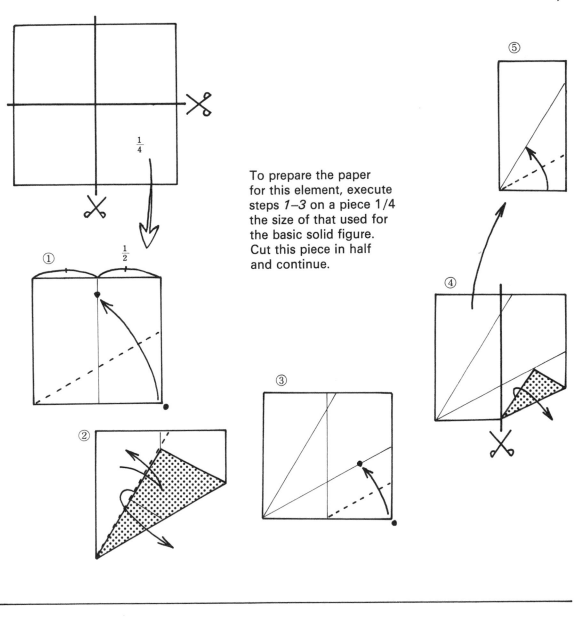

$\frac{1}{4}$

① $\frac{1}{2}$

② ③ ④ ⑤

To prepare the paper
for this element, execute
steps *1–3* on a piece 1/4
the size of that used for
the basic solid figure.
Cut this piece in half
and continue.

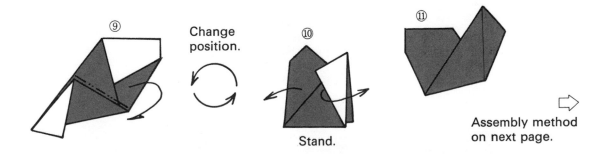

⑨

Change
position.

⑩

⑪

Stand.

Assembly method
on next page.

121

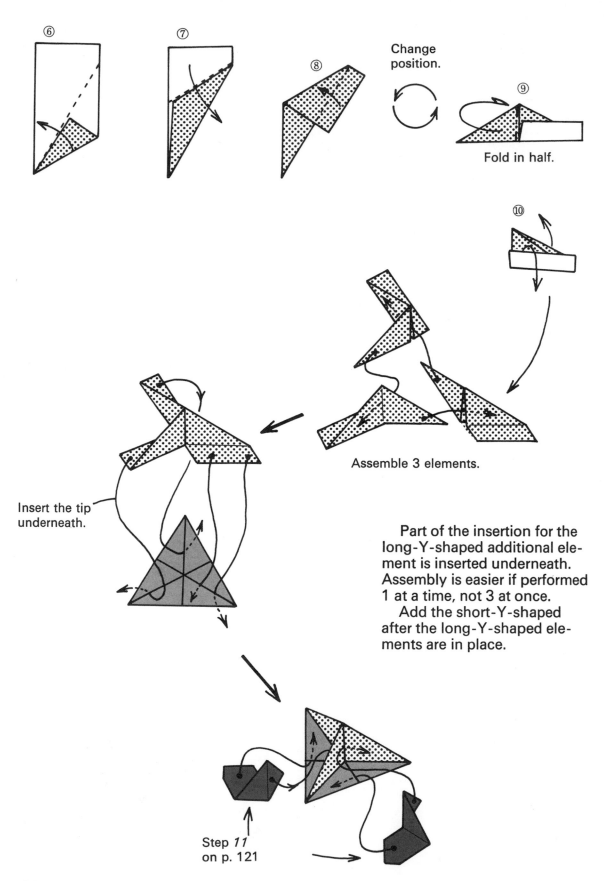

⑥

⑦

⑧

Change
position.

⑨

Fold in half.

⑩

Assemble 3 elements.

Insert the tip
underneath.

Part of the insertion for the
long-Y-shaped additional element is inserted underneath.
Assembly is easier if performed
1 at a time, not 3 at once.
Add the short-Y-shaped
after the long-Y-shaped elements are in place.

Step *11*
on p. 121

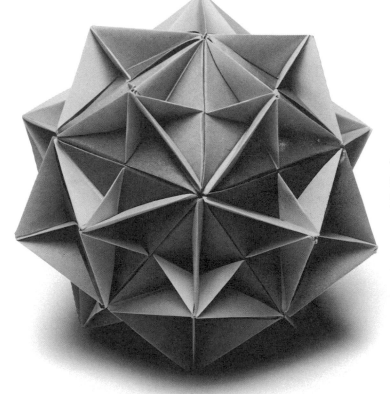

Regular icosahedron
20-unit assembly
decorated with Long-
Y-form Elements
No. 1

The solid figure in
the upper figure further
decorated with Short-
Y-form Elements
No. 2

Propeller Unit from an Equilateral Triangle

The propeller unit made from a square piece of paper lacked an insertion.
It is possible to make a more perfect unit if we do not insist on square paper.
All the parts will be the sizes shown below. Though most of the units in
this book begin with square paper, as this one proves, it is possible to start
with a different shape.

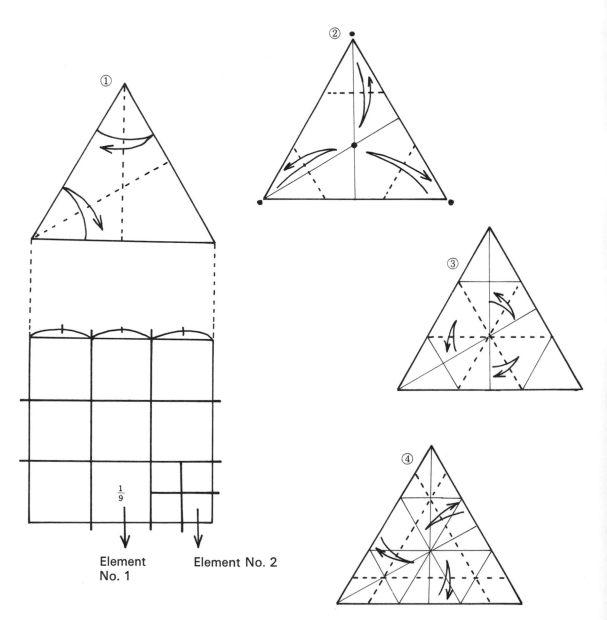

Element No. 1   Element No. 2

$\frac{1}{9}$

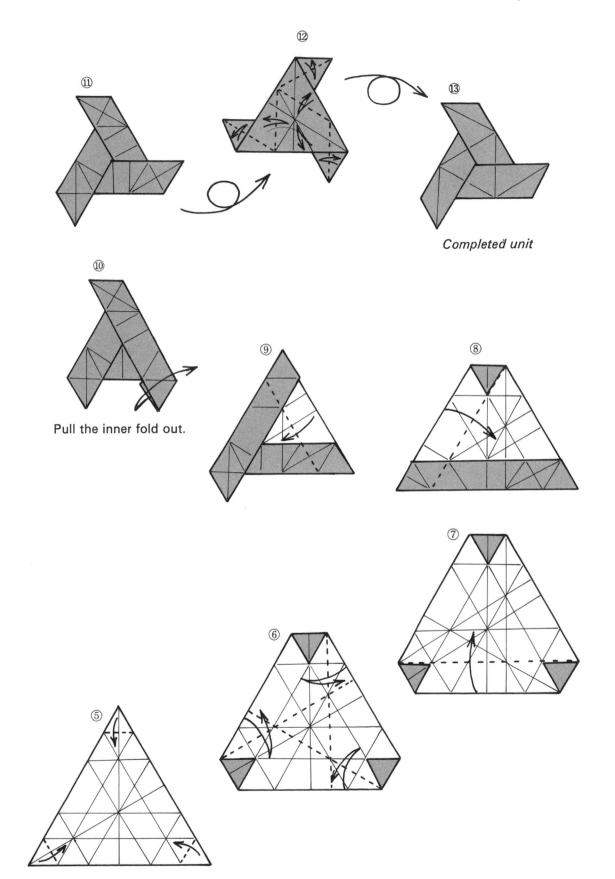

⑬

Completed unit

Pull the inner fold out.

125

Double-pocket Equilateral Triangles —Triangular Windows

As in the case of triangular windows (p. 104), this unit can be assembled in many ways. Here I explain the concave assembly. Assemblies are possible using both the upper and the under sides.

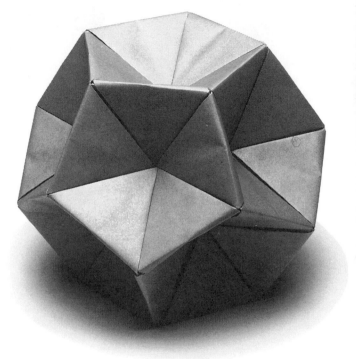

Dual triangles 30-unit concave standard assembly

① $\frac{1}{2}$

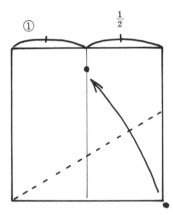

②

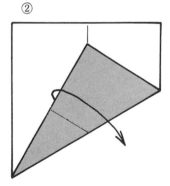

③

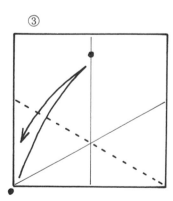

④

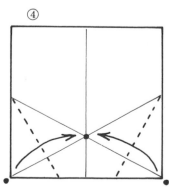

⑤

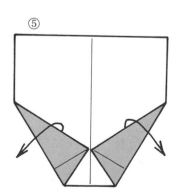

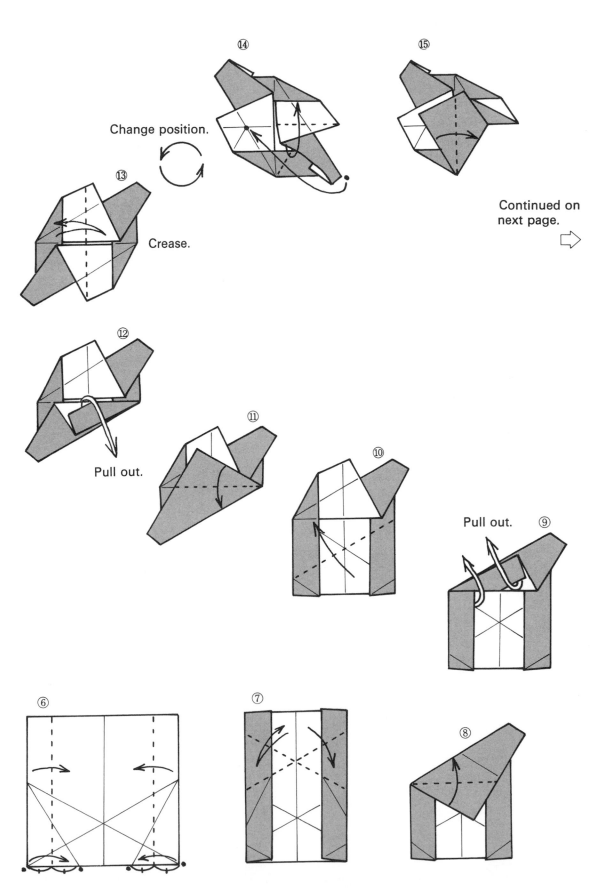

Change position.

Crease.

Continued on
next page.

Pull out.

Pull out.

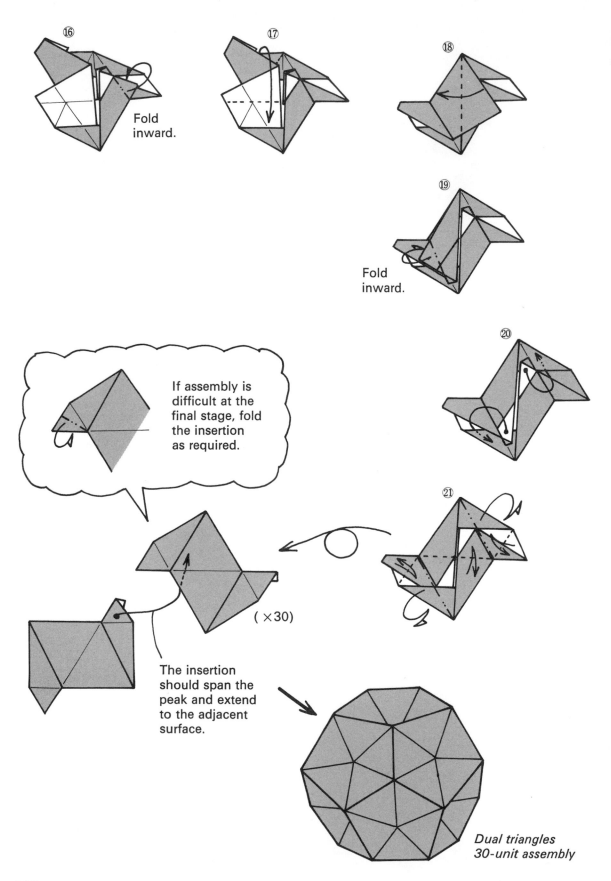

⑯ Fold inward.

⑰

⑱

⑲ Fold inward.

⑳

㉑

If assembly is difficult at the final stage, fold the insertion as required.

(×30)

The insertion should span the peak and extend to the adjacent surface.

Dual triangles 30-unit assembly

Dual triangles, reverse
assemblies of 12 (left),
4 (middle), and 30 (right)
units

In this slight alteration of the dual-
triangles unit, 30 units are assembled
to form the framework of a regular
icosahedron with a concavity in the
center. This unit can be inverted and
assembled as in the inset on the right.

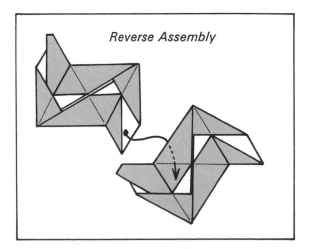

Reverse Assembly

Element No. 1

Inserting additional elements into the 5 radial slits in each concave surface of the solid figure shown on p. 128 produces a figure like the one in the photograph on the next page. Starlike forms fitted perfectly into the concavities amplify the figure's radiance.

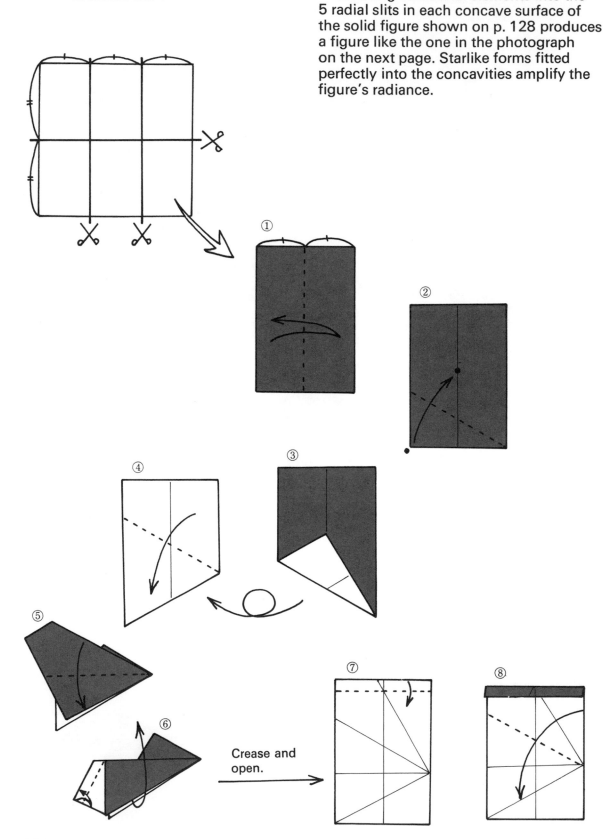

Crease and open.

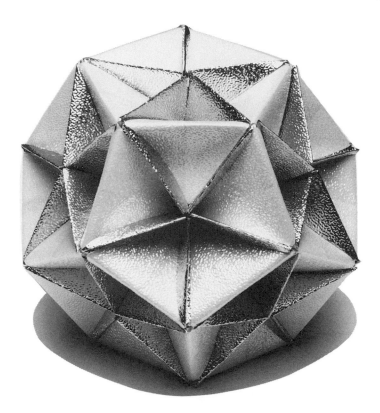

Elements No. 1 added to
the dual-triangle 30-unit
concave standard assembly

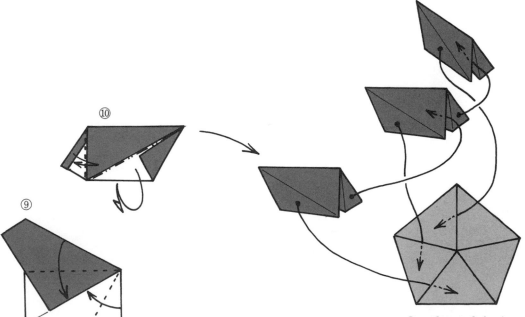

⑩

⑨

One face of dual-
triangular 30-unit
concave assembly

Origami Fate

Sometimes I burn origami that have been crushed or that prove unsuccessful in one way or another. As I watch the green, blue, and orange flames (probably caused by the pigments used to color the paper), I reflect on the sad ephemerality of those animal forms and starlike solid-geometric figures and on the time I spent engrossed in creating them.

The life of an origami reaches its zenith with the delight that glows in the face of its creator either at the instant of completion or at the moment when the work is offered as a gift to someone else. It is fated, however, to decline thereafter.

The life span of origami works of all kinds —animal and flower forms or unit-figures—is short. Displayed on shelf or table, they are the center of attention for a little while. Some of them serve for a time as containers. But, sooner or later, they becomes dusty, faded, and destined for the trash basket. Even carefully kept they do not remain in good condition very long.

Nonetheless, though the individual folded works may be short-lived, an origami design springs to fresh life each time someone executes it and in this sense may be regarded as eternal.

Chapter 5: Growing Polyhedrons

Up to this point, we have combined similar solid figures; that is, cubes with cubes, and so on. In this chapter, we allow polyhedrons to develop in all directions into space to generate new kinds of unit-origami solids.

Bird and Pinwheel Tetrahedron
3-unit Assembly (by Kunihiko Kasahara)

Folding the Bird Tetrahedron

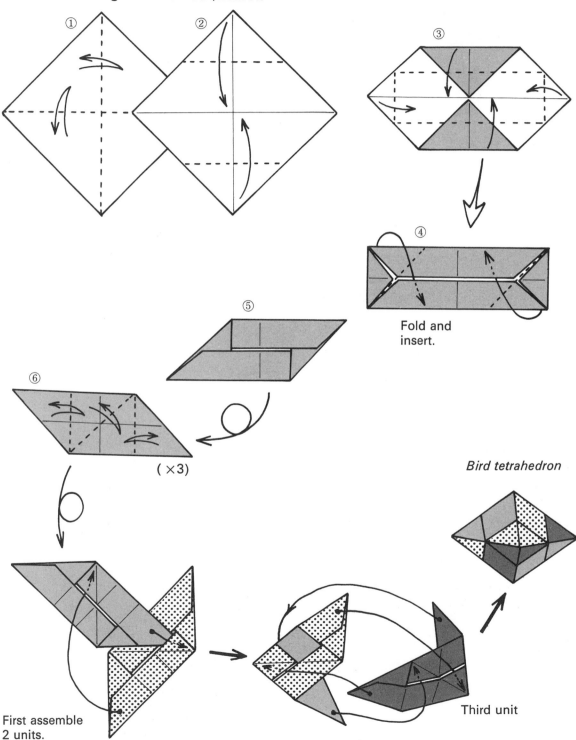

④ Fold and insert.

(×3)

First assemble 2 units.

Third unit

Bird tetrahedron

Folding the Pinwheel Tetrahedron

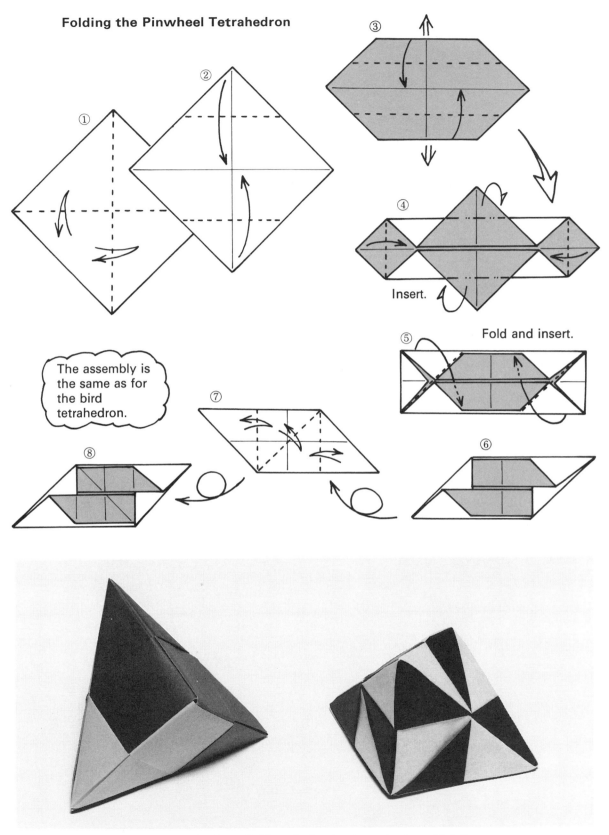

The assembly is the same as for the bird tetrahedron.

Insert.

Fold and insert.

Bird tetrahedron (left) and pinwheel tetrahedron (right)

135

Bird Cube 6-unit Assembly

(by Kunihiko Kasahara)

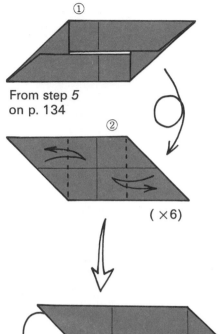

①

From step 5
on p. 134

②

(×6)

Their designer Kunihiko Kasahara has chris-
tened the cubes with the easy-to-remember
nicknames of bird and pinwheel because of
the patterns formed by creases and slits on
their surfaces. They and the simplified Sonobè
unit on p. 72 are well known.

Referring to "Polyhedrons Summarized"
on p. 238, work out various spherical assemblies
using the kinds of creases shown in the box
below.

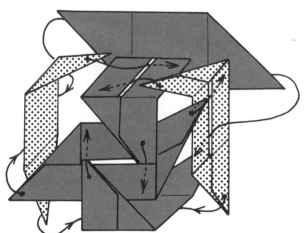

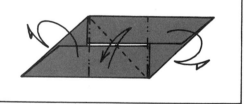

For a spherical assembly,
crease as shown here.

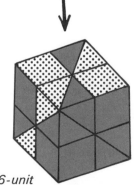

*Bird cube 6-unit
assembly*

Bird pattern

Appearing to wrap around
the cube edges, this com-
bination of squares and
triangles is the form that
gives the bird cube its name.

Pinwheel pattern

▲
Bird cube 6-unit
assembly (left) and
pinwheel cube 6-
unit assembly
(right)

▶
Bird 30-unit
assembly (top),
pinwheel 9-unit
assembly (middle),
and pinwheel 12-
unit assembly
(bottom)

Bird Tetrahedron 3-unit Assembly

Begin by assembling 3 bird tetrahedron
3-unit assembly (p. 134). Or you may
replace the bird tetrahedrons with pinwheel
tetrahedrons. Connect them vertically and
horizontally with the joints shown here.
Both the folding and the assembly are very
simple.

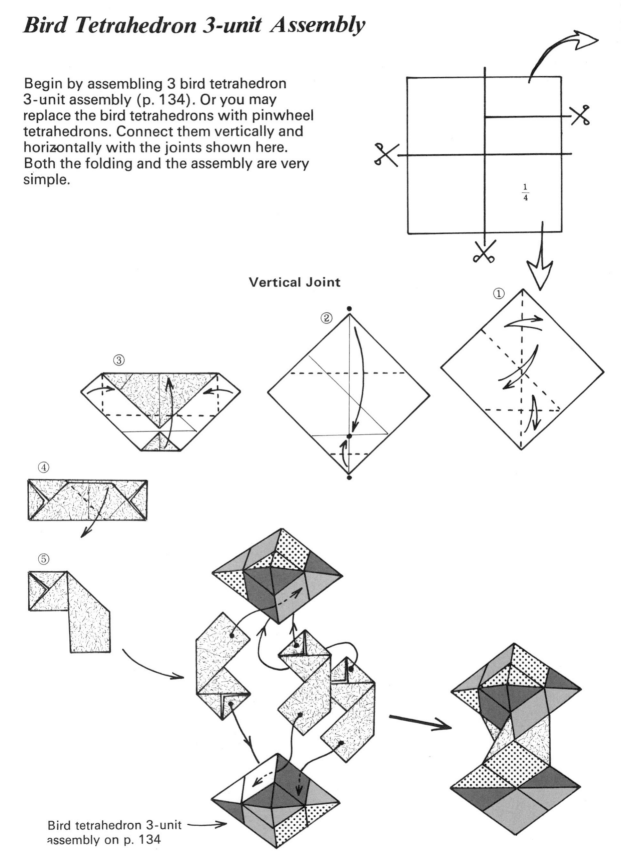

Vertical Joint

Bird tetrahedron 3-unit
assembly on p. 134

Joint No. 1 for Horizontal Connection of 3-unit Assembly

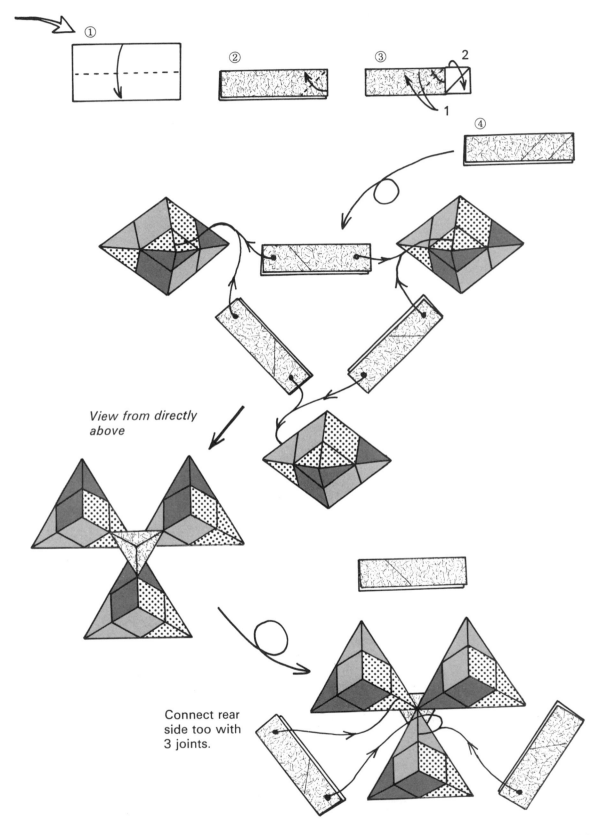

① ② ③ ④

View from directly above

Connect rear side too with 3 joints.

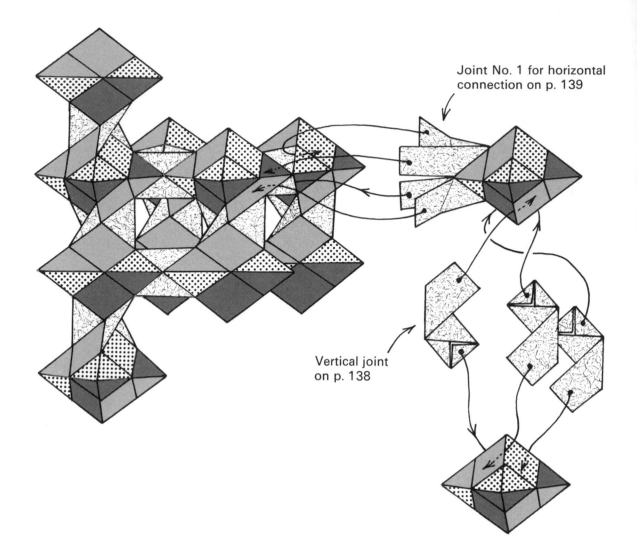

Joint No. 1 for horizontal connection on p. 139

Vertical joint on p. 138

A Special Kind of Pleasure

I was delighted to discover the use of the slits and insertions discussed earlier in this book but was struck dumb by the discovery of this connecting method. I had to calm myself a while before I felt able to try it out. Then, when I realized that it works more easily and smoothly than I had hoped and makes possible strong combinations of numbers of units, I experienced a very special kind of pleasure that only unit origami can give.

The slit-and-insertion method enables us to perform a limitless kind of reproduction-reproduction similar to cellular fission. This joining system makes possible dynamic, free growth. Having revealed this trump —the ultimate in novelty —unit origami still probably has more cards to play.

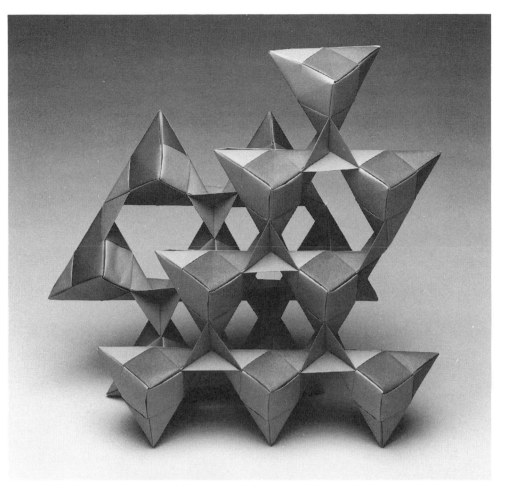

Bird tetrahedron 3-unit assemblies joined by means of Joint No. 1

The construction above seen from a different angle

Joint No. 2 for Horizontal Connection of 3-unit Assembly

This 3-unit assembly does not employ the same slits as those used in the preceding assembly. If joints seem frail, use double-layer paper. The same is true with vertical joints.

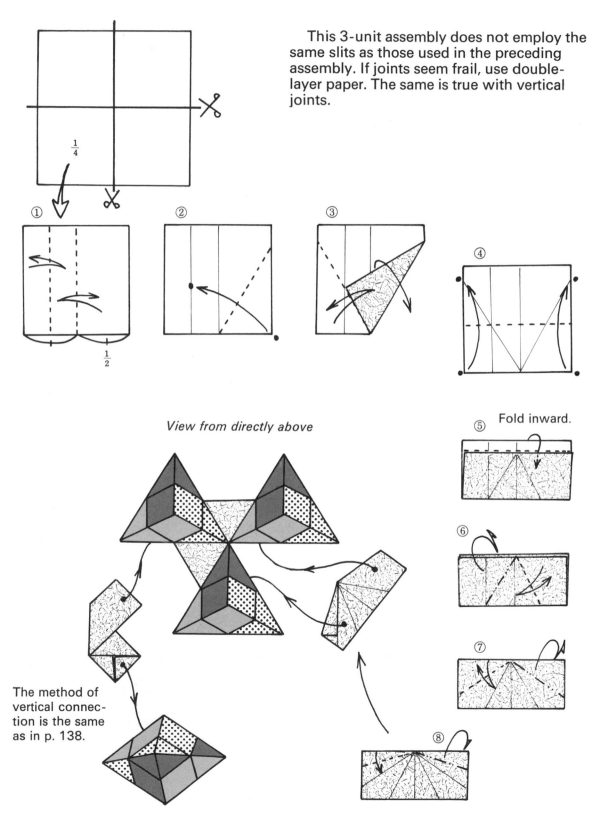

$\frac{1}{4}$

①

$\frac{1}{2}$

②

③

④

View from directly above

⑤ Fold inward.

⑥

⑦

The method of vertical connection is the same as in p. 138.

⑧

Pinwheel tetra-
hedron 3-unit
assemblies
joined by
means of Joint
No. 2

The construc-
tion above seen
from a different
angle

Joint No. 1 for Horizontal Connection of 2-unit Assembly

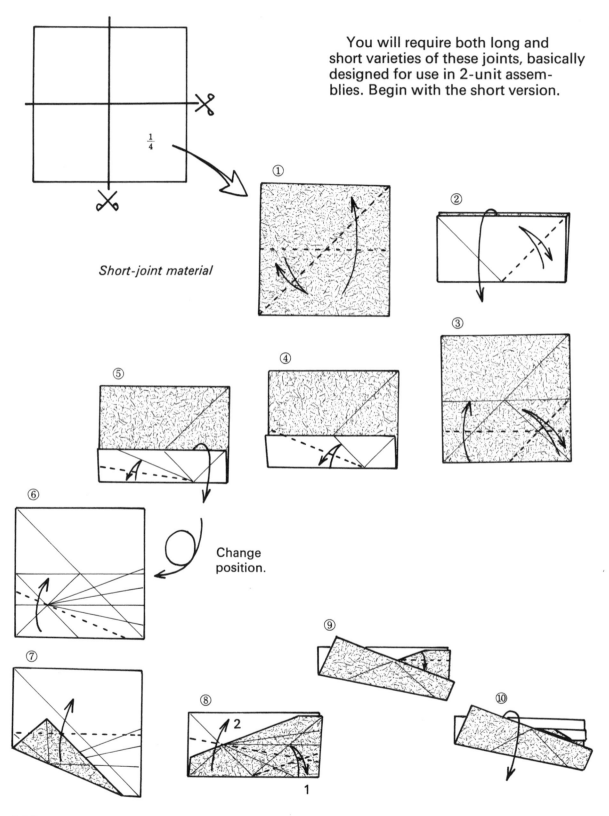

You will require both long and short varieties of these joints, basically designed for use in 2-unit assemblies. Begin with the short version.

$\frac{1}{4}$

Short-joint material

Change position.

144

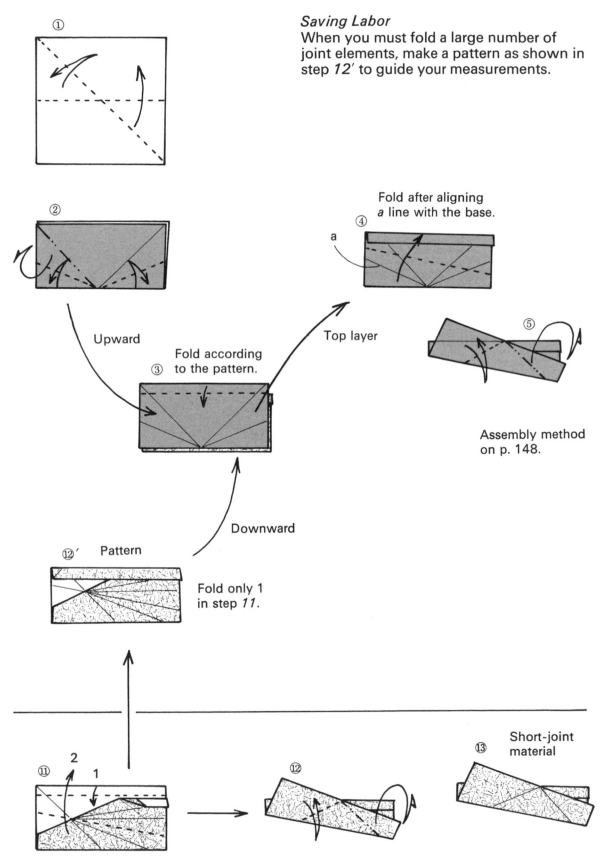

①

Saving Labor
When you must fold a large number of
joint elements, make a pattern as shown in
step *12'* to guide your measurements.

②

Fold after aligning
a line with the base.
④

a

Upward

Fold according
③ to the pattern.

Top layer

⑤

Assembly method
on p. 148.

Downward

⑫' Pattern

Fold only 1
in step *11*.

Short-joint
⑬ material

⑪

2
1

⑫

Joint No. 2 for Horizontal Connection of 2-unit Assembly

This makes a big difference with a 3-unit assembly.

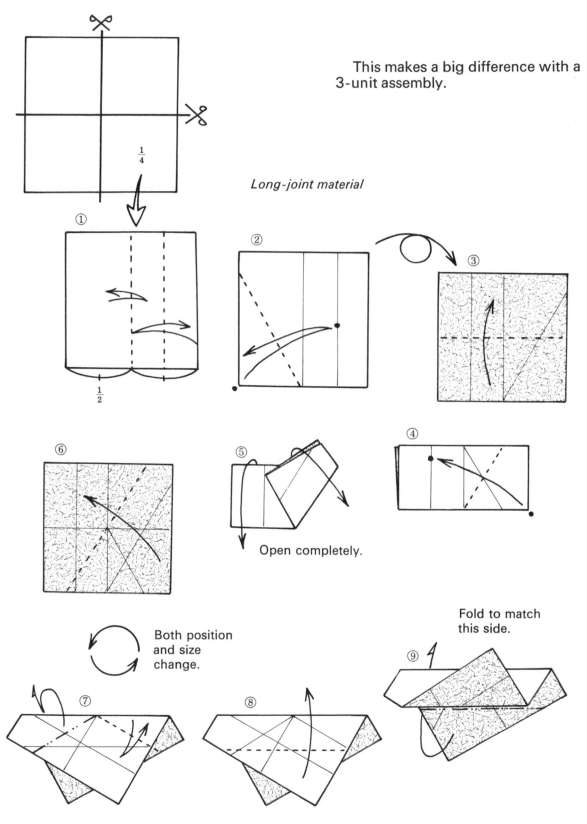

$\frac{1}{4}$

Long-joint material

①

$\frac{1}{2}$

②

③

④

⑤

Open completely.

⑥

Both position and size change.

⑦

⑧

⑨

Fold to match this side.

Lateral view of a construction made of bird tetrahedron 3-unit assemblies connected by means of long- and short-joint materials

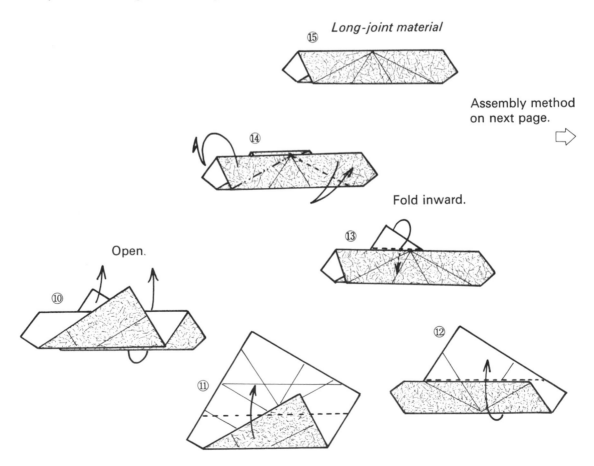

Long-joint material

⑮

Assembly method on next page. ⇨

⑭

Fold inward.

⑬

Open.

⑩

⑪

⑫

147

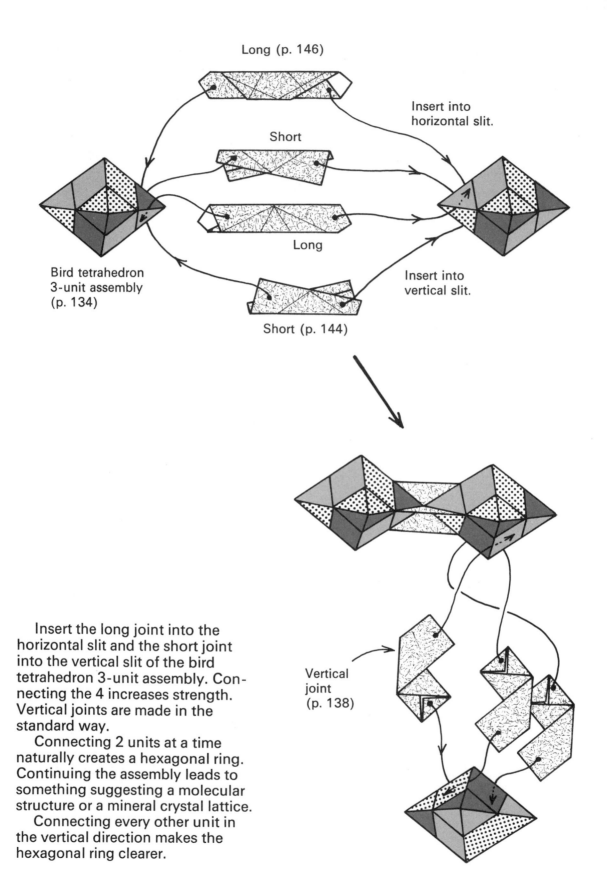

Long (p. 146)

Short

Long

Bird tetrahedron
3-unit assembly
(p. 134)

Short (p. 144)

Insert into
horizontal slit.

Insert into
vertical slit.

Insert the long joint into the
horizontal slit and the short joint
into the vertical slit of the bird
tetrahedron 3-unit assembly. Connecting the 4 increases strength.
Vertical joints are made in the
standard way.

Connecting 2 units at a time
naturally creates a hexagonal ring.
Continuing the assembly leads to
something suggesting a molecular
structure or a mineral crystal lattice.

Connecting every other unit in
the vertical direction makes the
hexagonal ring clearer.

Vertical
joint
(p. 138)

The construction on p. 147 viewed from a different angle. On the left is a triple-group.

Joining a Pinwheel-cube 6-unit Assembly

This same method may be used with the bird cube too. Inserting joints in edge slits makes it possible to join the corners of cubes. Each joint of the No. 1 kind is inserted into 1 slit only. Since the joints are easy to fold and fit the slits smoothly, you will probably want to connect many solid figures this way.

$\frac{1}{4}$

Joint No. 1

①

②

Rearward

Pinwheel cube 6-unit assembly on p. 136

Downward

To the side

Open edge

In connecting take care that the open edge of the joint is concealed.

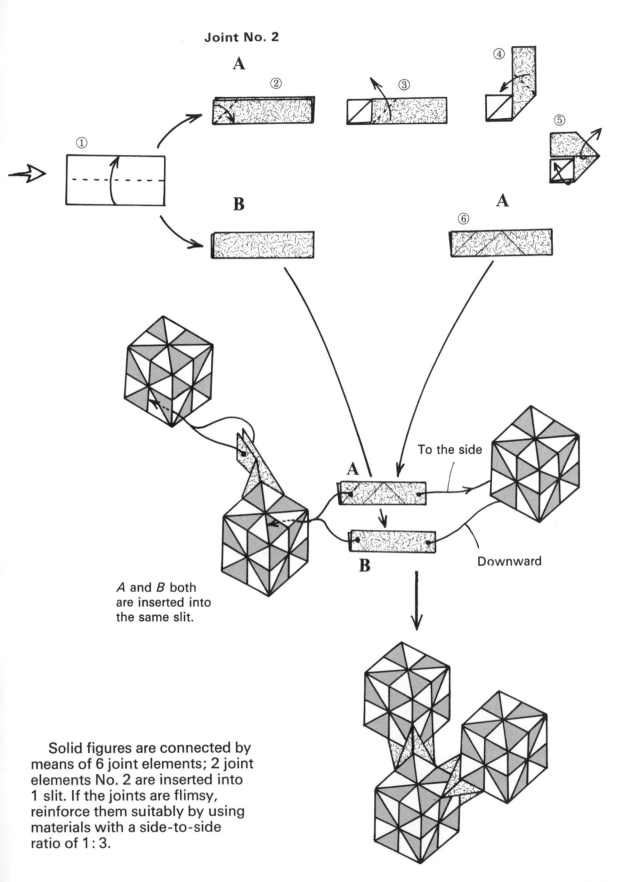

Joint No. 2

A

B

A

B

To the side

Downward

A and B both
are inserted into
the same slit.

Solid figures are connected by
means of 6 joint elements; 2 joint
elements No. 2 are inserted into
1 slit. If the joints are flimsy,
reinforce them suitably by using
materials with a side-to-side
ratio of 1 : 3.

Bird cube 6-unit assemblies
connected by means of
Joints No. 1

Theoretically all the examples given in this chapter may be expanded infinitely with further connections. Actually, however, the weight of the solid body and the strength of the joints impose limitations. Although I have not yet challenged a large assembly, it would be interesting to know just how far it is possible to go. If it is too much work for a single person, call on your family and friends for help in creating entertaining and beautiful works that exceed many people's expectations of origami.

Three bird cubes connected by means of Joint No. 1

Pinwheel cube 6-unit assemblies connected by means of Joints No. 2

Dual Triangles

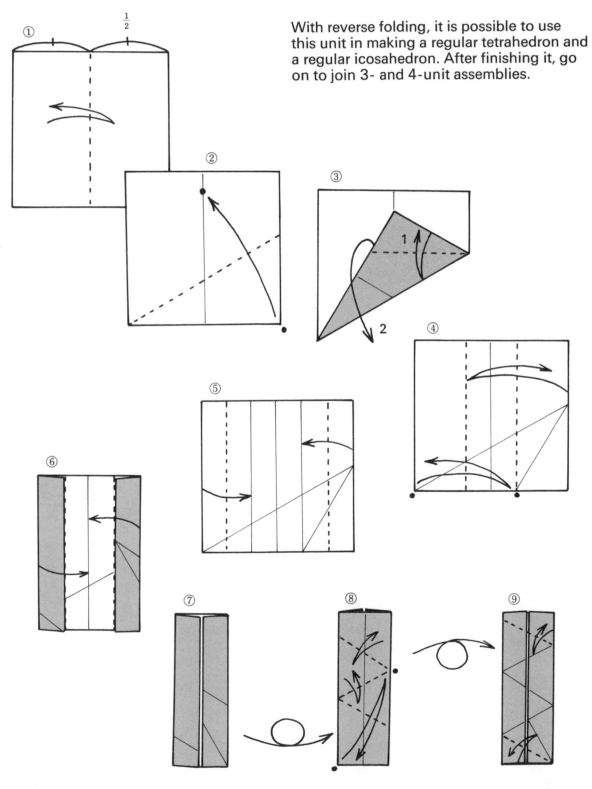

With reverse folding, it is possible to use this unit in making a regular tetrahedron and a regular icosahedron. After finishing it, go on to join 3- and 4-unit assemblies.

Regular octahedron 4-unit assembly (left), regular tetrahedron 3-unit assembly (middle), and regular icosahedron 10-unit assembly (right)

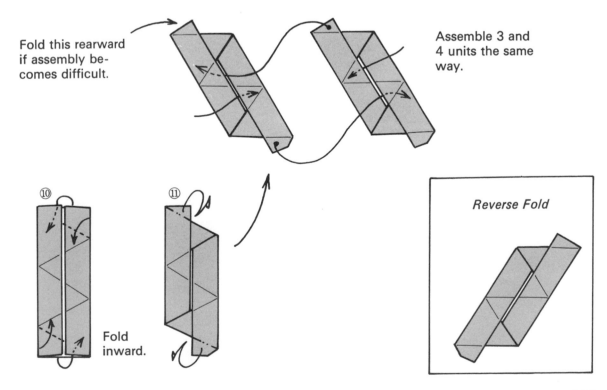

Fold this rearward if assembly becomes difficult.

Assemble 3 and 4 units the same way.

⑩

⑪

Fold inward.

Reverse Fold

155

Joining 3 Dual Triangles

Deciding which of the 2 vertical slits to use is
a problem. The junction is firmer if the insertion is made in a slit that is part of a unit instead
of one between units.

　As was the case with the bird and pinwheel
tetrahedron 3-unit assemblies, a natural
twist develops in the vertical direction.
This twist provides entertaining variety. Part
of origami's charm lies in such uncalculated
developments.

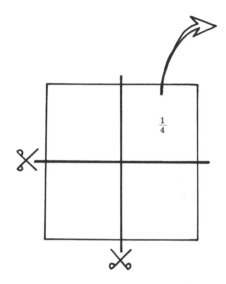

156

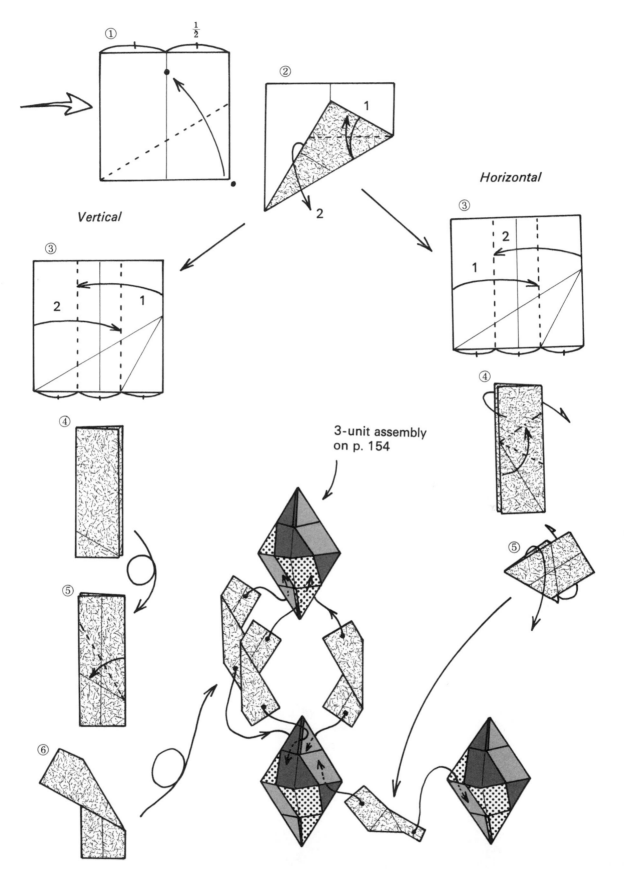

① $\frac{1}{2}$

② 1 2

Vertical

③ 2 1

④

⑤

⑥

Horizontal

③ 2 1

④

⑤

3-unit assembly
on p. 154

Joining 4 Dual Triangles

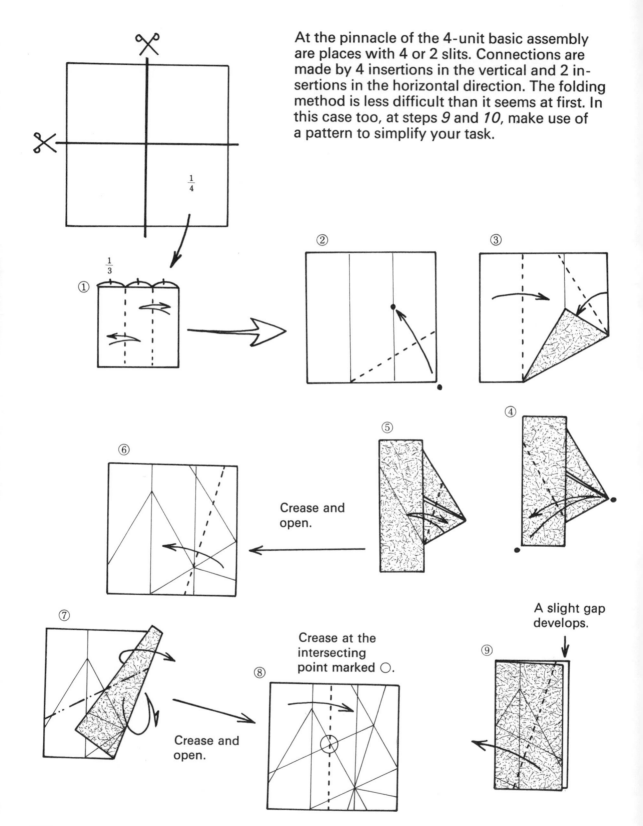

At the pinnacle of the 4-unit basic assembly are places with 4 or 2 slits. Connections are made by 4 insertions in the vertical and 2 insertions in the horizontal direction. The folding method is less difficult than it seems at first. In this case too, at steps *9* and *10*, make use of a pattern to simplify your task.

$\frac{1}{4}$

$\frac{1}{3}$

① ② ③ ④ ⑤

Crease and open.

⑥ ⑦

Crease and open.

Crease at the intersecting point marked ○.

⑧

A slight gap develops.

⑨

158

4-unit assembly
on p. 154

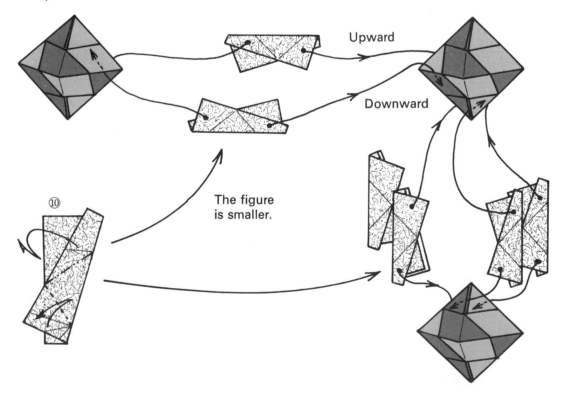

Upward

Downward

⑩

The figure
is smaller.

Dual Wedges

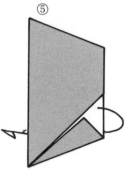

Dual wedge assemblies of 12 (left) and 6 (right) units

The length of a side of the square becomes the length of the unit. Use slightly small paper if you intend to employ the connection method shown on p. 164.

In the *A* assembly method, the wedge is visible; in the *B* assembly, it is not.

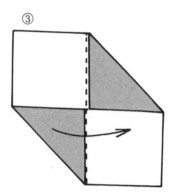

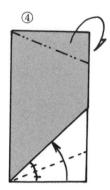

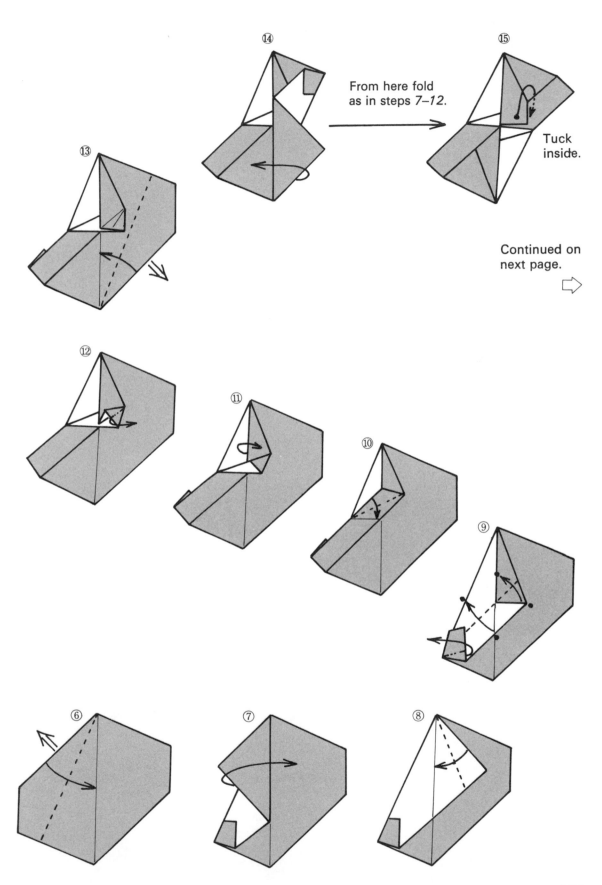

⑭

From here fold
as in steps *7–12*.

⑮

Tuck
inside.

Continued on
next page.

⑬

⑫

⑪

⑩

⑨

⑥

⑦

⑧

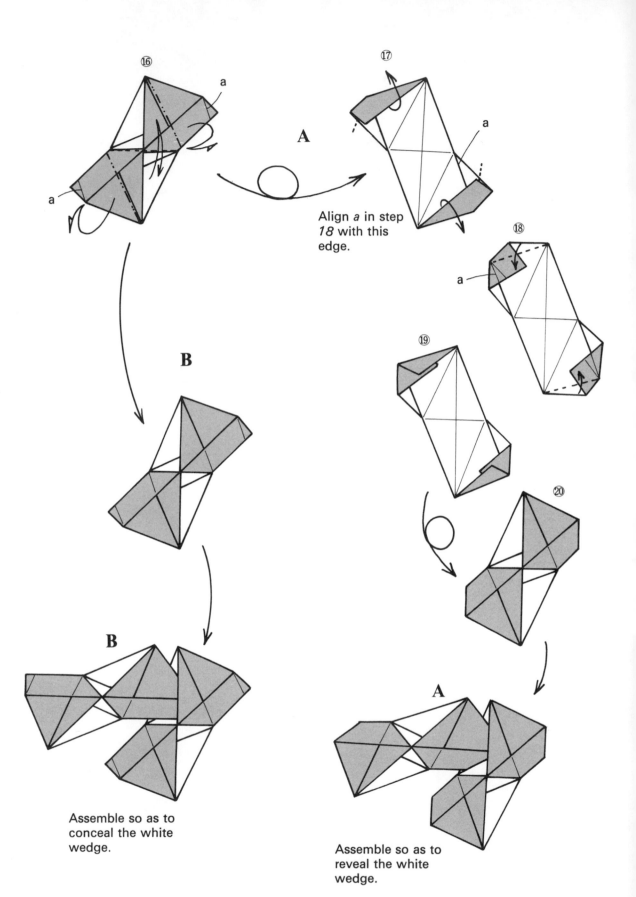

⑯ a a

A

Align *a* in step *18* with this edge.

⑰ a a

⑱ a

⑲

⑳

B

B

Assemble so as to conceal the white wedge.

A

Assemble so as to reveal the white wedge.

The *A* method used with a 24-unit assembly (left) and with a 6-unit assembly (right)

There are many varieties of assembling methods. Next connect 6-unit assemblies.

The *B* method used with a 21-unit assembly (left) and the *A* method used with a 3-unit assembly (right)

Connecting 6 Dual Wedges

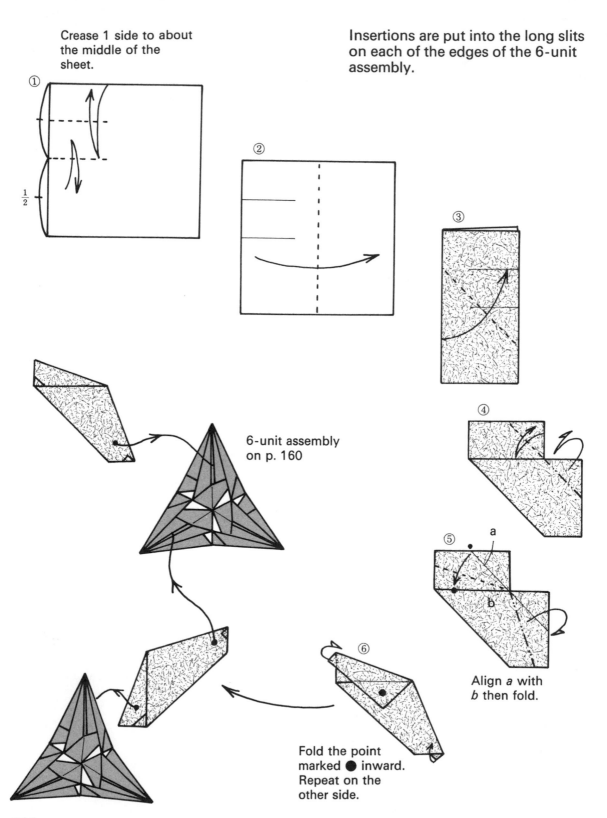

Crease 1 side to about the middle of the sheet.

① $\frac{1}{2}$

②

Insertions are put into the long slits on each of the edges of the 6-unit assembly.

③

④

⑤ a b

Align *a* with *b* then fold.

6-unit assembly on p. 160

⑥

Fold the point marked ● inward. Repeat on the other side.

164

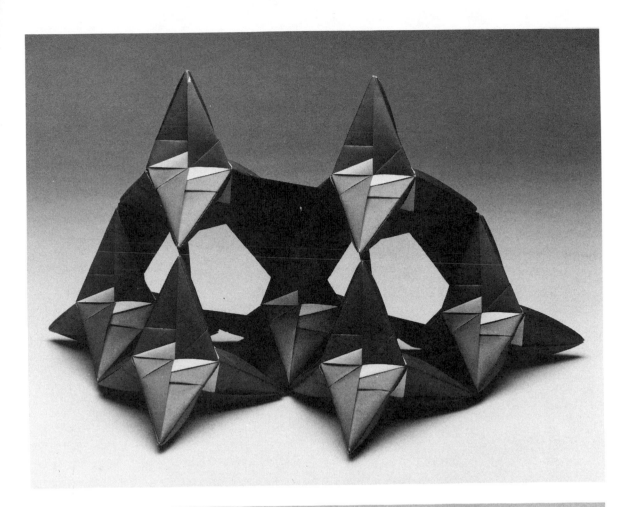

This connecting methods is slightly weaker than the others. You will probably have more fun folding with a different kind of joint or with a new unit with different slits.

On Not Giving up

I am sometimes troubled to hear people complain that the works I explain are much too difficult to fold. The complaint usually comes, not from devoted origami fans, but from people who suddenly take up origami again as a nostalgic reminder of their childhoods. Concerned by their plight, I advise them not to give up but to keep folding, even if only one more time.

Anyone can fold origami, but it is necessary to get used to the methods and learn the best ways. The difficulties of unit origami can be irritating. I rarely fold another person's new work perfectly the first time. My initial version is usually wrinkled and messy, but I master the difficulties the second or third time.

Since I do not want to lose new origami friends, I try to make certain that the works I offer are interesting enough to justify your perseverance and ask that, when difficulty arises, you stick to the problem till you have overcome it. Perhaps my worry is excessive. I certainly hope so.

Chapter 6: Simple Variations

In this chapter, additions are made to basic solid figures, solid figures are joined together, and some simple tricks are used to make big differences.

Windowed Units—Muff

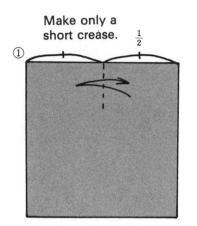

Make only a short crease.

$\frac{1}{2}$

In addition to the pockets, this unit has slits on both edges to make it possible to produce something like the muffs in which ladies once kept their hands warm.

Variations *A* and *B* result from slight changes in the folding method of the same 6-unit assembly. Both produce solid figures with windowlike openings.

In addition to leaving it as it is, you may add elements. Doing this changes the form as if by magic.

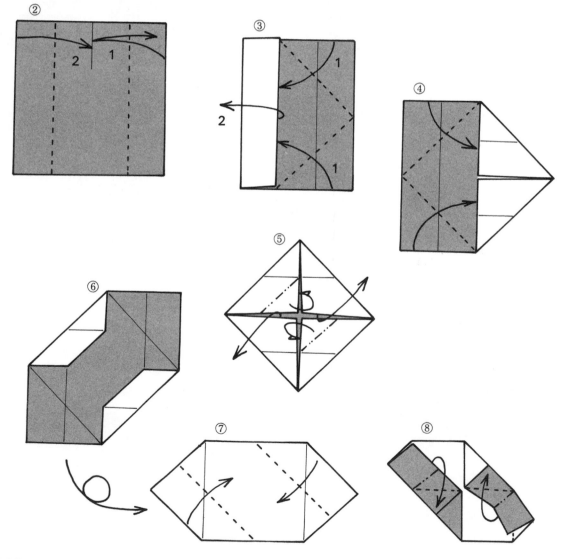

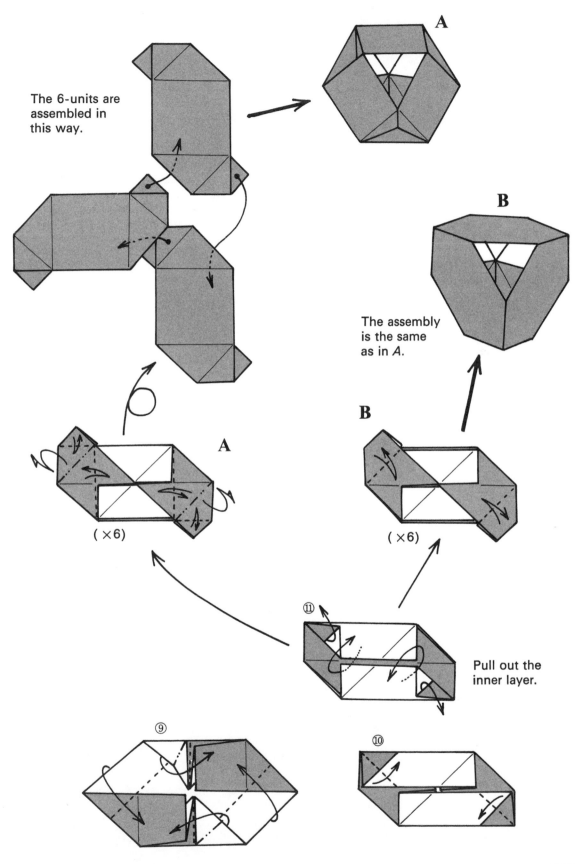

The 6-units are
assembled in
this way.

A

B

The assembly
is the same
as in *A*.

A

(×6)

B

(×6)

⑪

Pull out the
inner layer.

⑨

⑩

Variation I

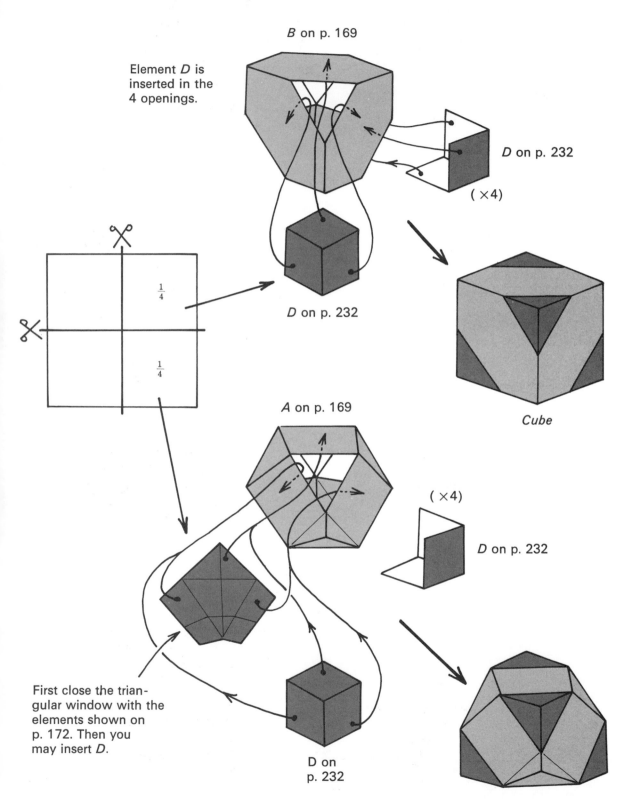

B on p. 169

Element *D* is inserted in the 4 openings.

D on p. 232

(×4)

$\frac{1}{4}$

$\frac{1}{4}$

D on p. 232

Cube

A on p. 169

(×4)

D on p. 232

First close the triangular window with the elements shown on p. 172. Then you may insert *D*.

D on p. 232

On the left is a 6-unit-*A* assembly; on the right, the same figure plus *D*.

On the left is a 6-unit-*B* assembly; on the right, the same figure plus *D*.

Variation II

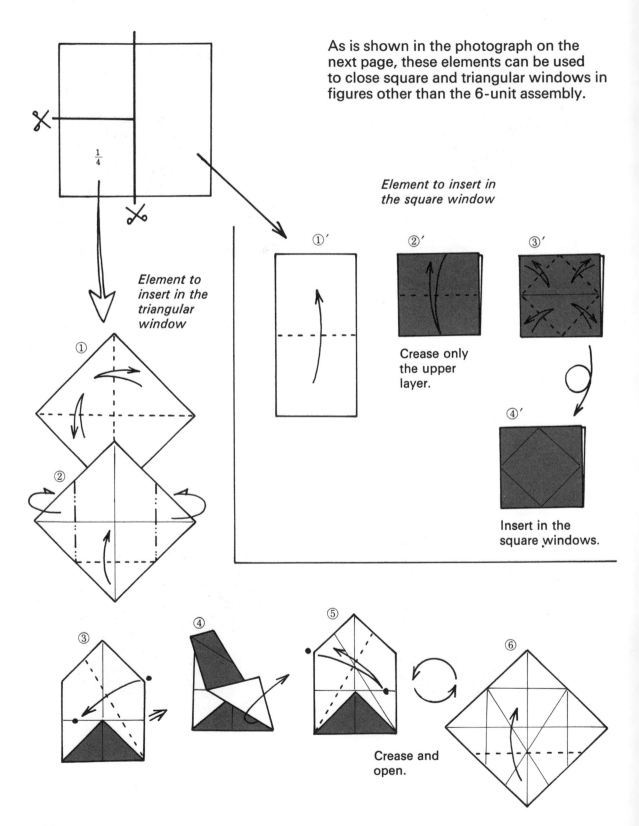

As is shown in the photograph on the next page, these elements can be used to close square and triangular windows in figures other than the 6-unit assembly.

$\frac{1}{4}$

Element to insert in the triangular window

Element to insert in the square window

①′

②′

Crease only the upper layer.

③′

④′

Insert in the square windows.

①

②

③

④

⑤

Crease and open.

⑥

On the left is a 6-unit-*A* assembly plus Element No. 1; on the right is a 12-unit-*B* assembly plus Element No. 2

B on p. 169

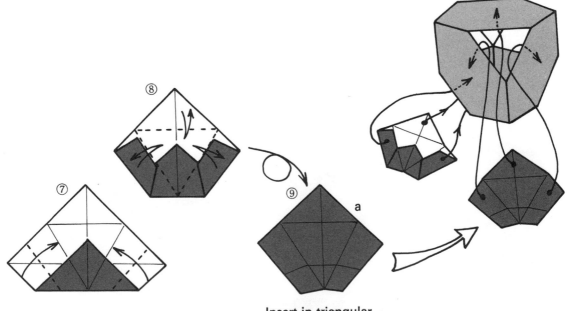

⑦ ⑧ ⑨ a

Insert in triangular windows.

Connecting 6 Windowed Units

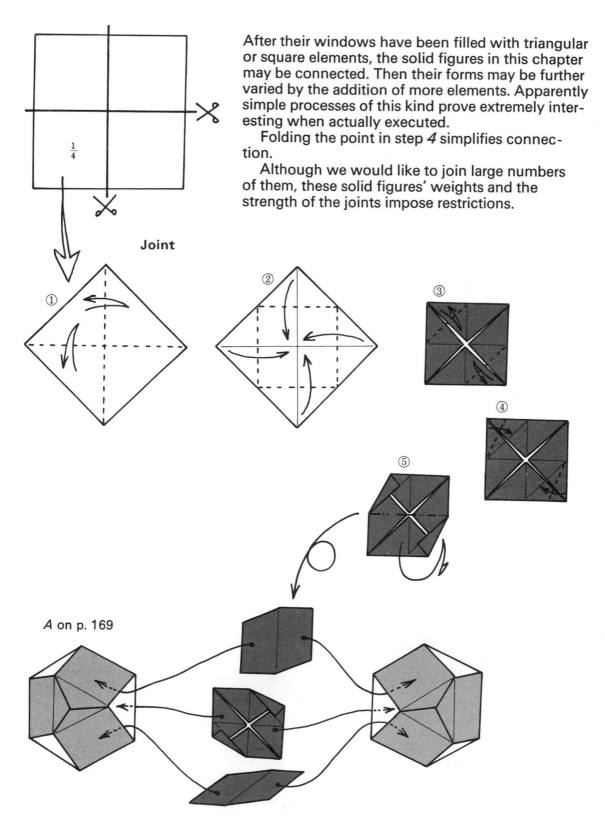

After their windows have been filled with triangular or square elements, the solid figures in this chapter may be connected. Then their forms may be further varied by the addition of more elements. Apparently simple processes of this kind prove extremely interesting when actually executed.

Folding the point in step *4* simplifies connection.

Although we would like to join large numbers of them, these solid figures' weights and the strength of the joints impose restrictions.

$\frac{1}{4}$

Joint

① ② ③ ④ ⑤

A on p. 169

After *D* were appended to the *A* assembly, 2 of the resulting figures were connected.

After Elements No. 2 were appended to the *B* assembly, 3 of the resulting figures were connected.

Large Square Flat Unit

Because of the simplicity of the work, in 2 places you are instructed to "fold as much as you like." Although it takes 2 pieces of paper to make, the unit is actually easy enough for anyone; and its surfaces are crease-free.

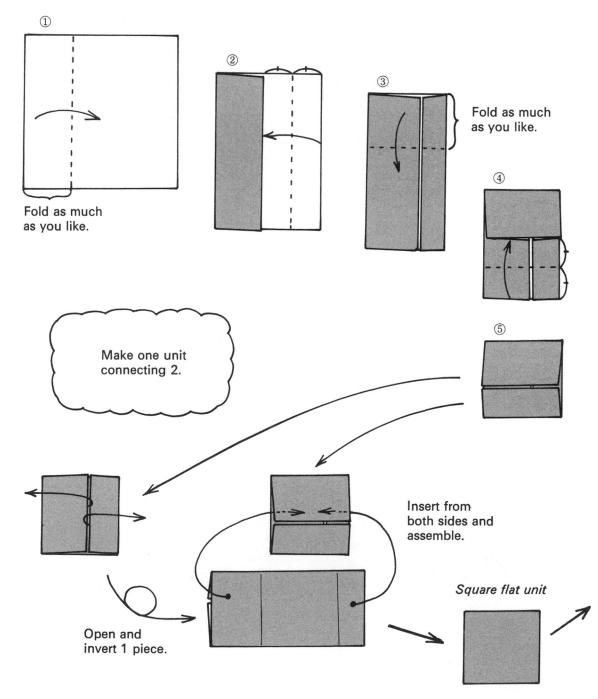

① Fold as much as you like.

②

③ Fold as much as you like.

④

⑤

Make one unit connecting 2.

Insert from both sides and assemble.

Open and invert 1 piece.

Square flat unit

Cube (right) and intermediary stage of assembly (left)

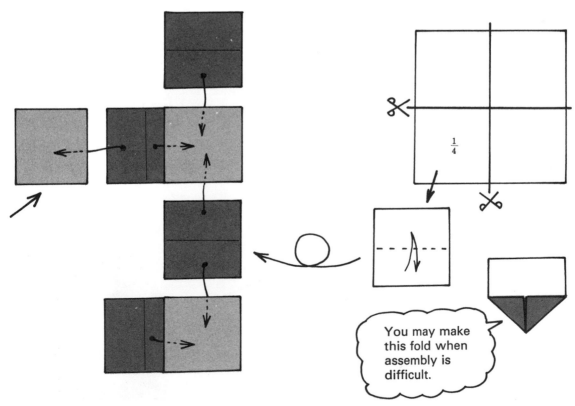

Joint

You may make this fold when assembly is difficult.

Transformation of Cuboctahedron I
Cuboctahedron → Cube

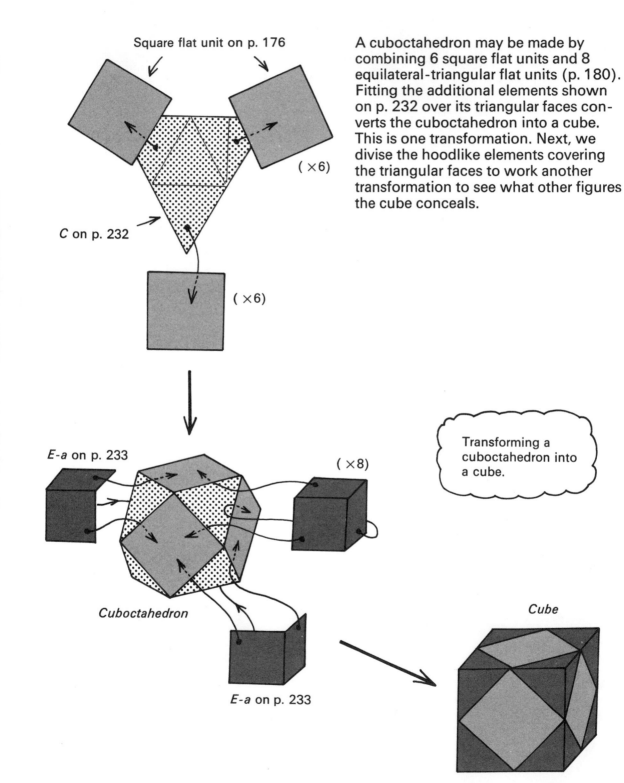

Square flat unit on p. 176

(×6)

C on p. 232

(×6)

E-a on p. 233

(×8)

Cuboctahedron

E-a on p. 233

Cube

A cuboctahedron may be made by combining 6 square flat units and 8 equilateral-triangular flat units (p. 180). Fitting the additional elements shown on p. 232 over its triangular faces converts the cuboctahedron into a cube. This is one transformation. Next, we divise the hoodlike elements covering the triangular faces to work another transformation to see what other figures the cube conceals.

Transforming a cuboctahedron into a cube.

With the joint elements shown on p. 177 it is possible to make a figure resembling 2 joined cuboctahedrons (upper photograph). Removing 1 element *C* converts the figure into a jug with a triangular mouth.

Removing the elements from the cube on the left produces the cuboctahedron.

Equilateral-triangular Flat Unit

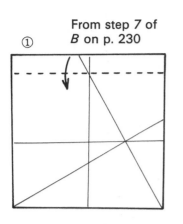

From step 7 of
B on p. 230

①

This unit has a wide application as a square flat unit. The joint shown on the next page is slightly weak. Unless glue is used, large constructions employing it tend to come apart.

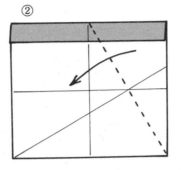

②

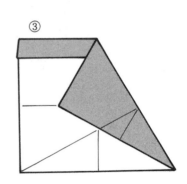

③

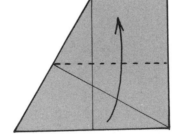

④

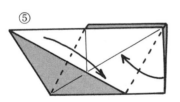

⑤

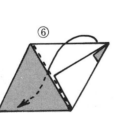

⑥

Tuck inside.

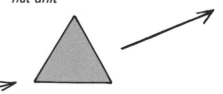

*Equilateral-triangular
flat unit*

Regular octahedron (left)
and regular icosahedron
(right)

Joint No. 1

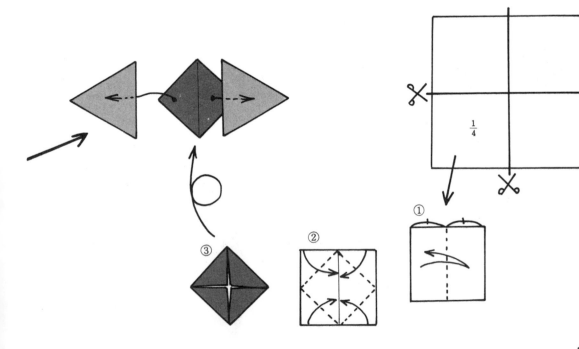

① ② ③

$\frac{1}{4}$

Transformation of Cuboctahedron II
Cuboctahedron → Regular Octahedron

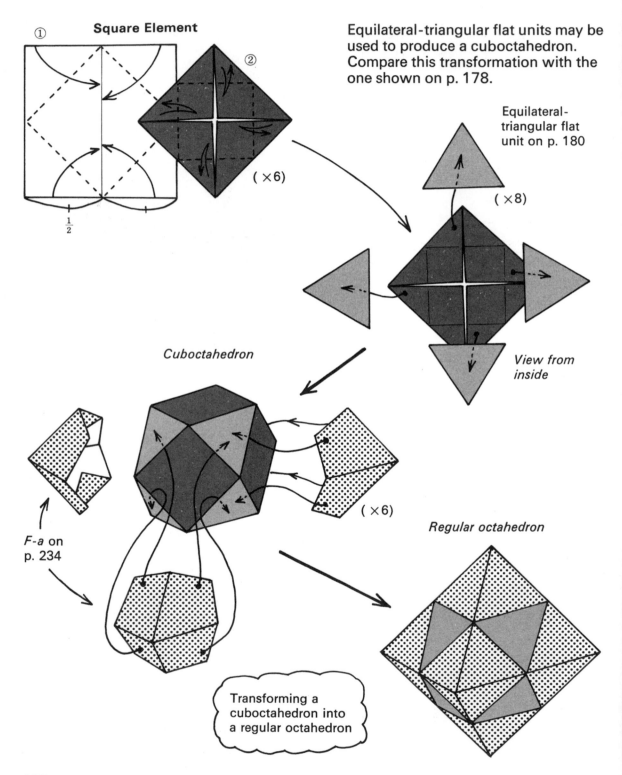

Square Element

① ②

(×6)

$\frac{1}{2}$

Equilateral-triangular flat units may be used to produce a cuboctahedron. Compare this transformation with the one shown on p. 178.

Equilateral-triangular flat unit on p. 180

(×8)

View from inside

Cuboctahedron

(×6)

F-a on p. 234

Regular octahedron

Transforming a cuboctahedron into a regular octahedron

This jug has a square mouth. Compare it with the one mentioned on p. 179. Of course, this one too can be combined into a long, slender jug. But in such a case, the assembly is slightly weak.

Adding the elements in the center to the cuboctahedron on the left produces the regular octahedron on the right.

Assembling Square Flat and Equilateral-triangular Flat Units

Joint No. 2

$\frac{1}{4}$

① ② ③

In this instance, the equilateral-triangular and the large square (p. 176) flat units are used together. Once again, the joints are troublesomely weak. I should be happy if my readers would devise better ones that are easy to use and require no glue.

Square flat unit on p. 176

Equilateral-triangular flat unit on p. 180

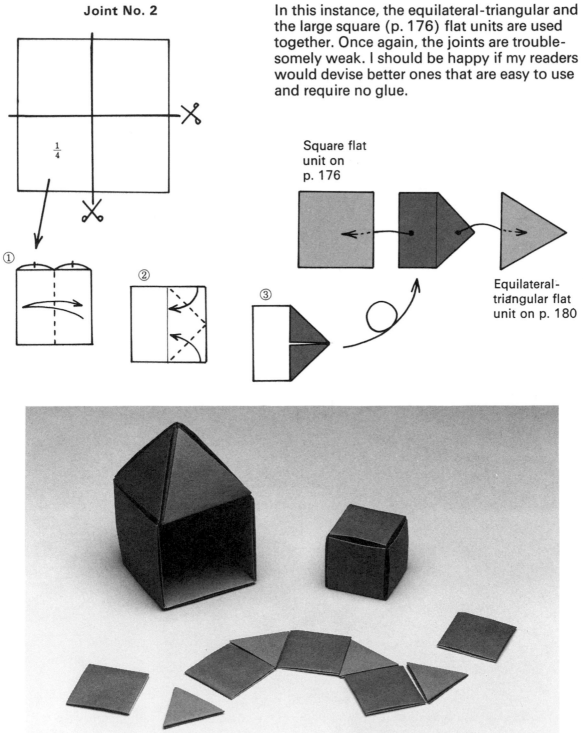

Transformation of Regular Octahedron I
Regular Octahedron → Regular Tetrahedron

Equilateral-
triangular flat
unit on p. 180

Adding hoodlike elements miracul-
ously transforms a regular octahedron
into a regular tetrahedron. This is
done all at once; next let us sub-
divide the transformation into
stages.

(×4)

(×4)   *C* on p. 232

*Regular
octahedron*

F-a on
p. 234

(×4)

*Regular
tetrahedron*

Transforming a
regular octahedron
into a regular
tetrahedron

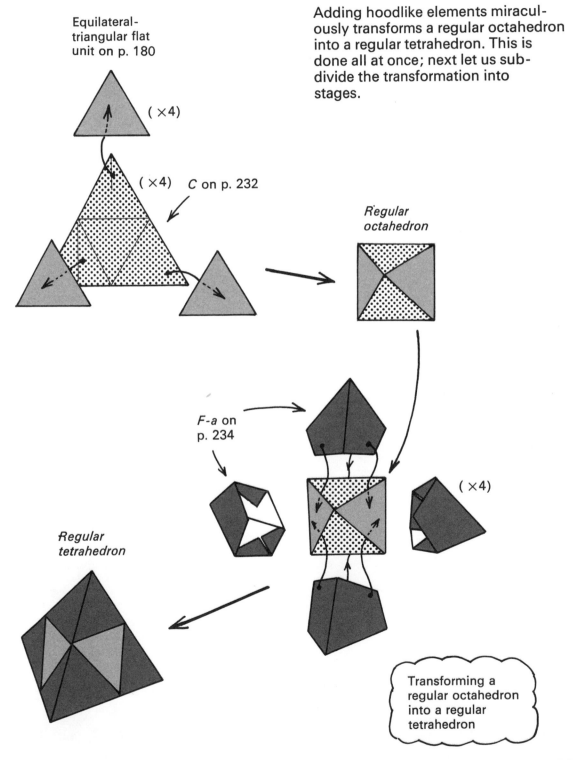

Transformation of Regular Octahedron II
Regular Octahedron → Truncated Tetrahedron

From step *7* of
B on p. 230

The basis is a regular octahedron. Adding 2 elements converts it into a truncated tetrahedron. After making creases for Element No. 1, cut it in two and use both halves. The folding methods for steps *3* and *4* differ between the left and right halves, but otherwise everything is the same.

Element No. 1

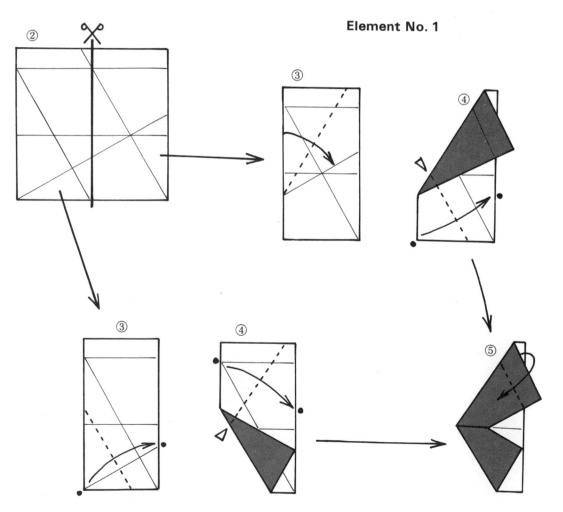
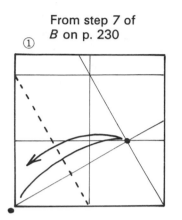

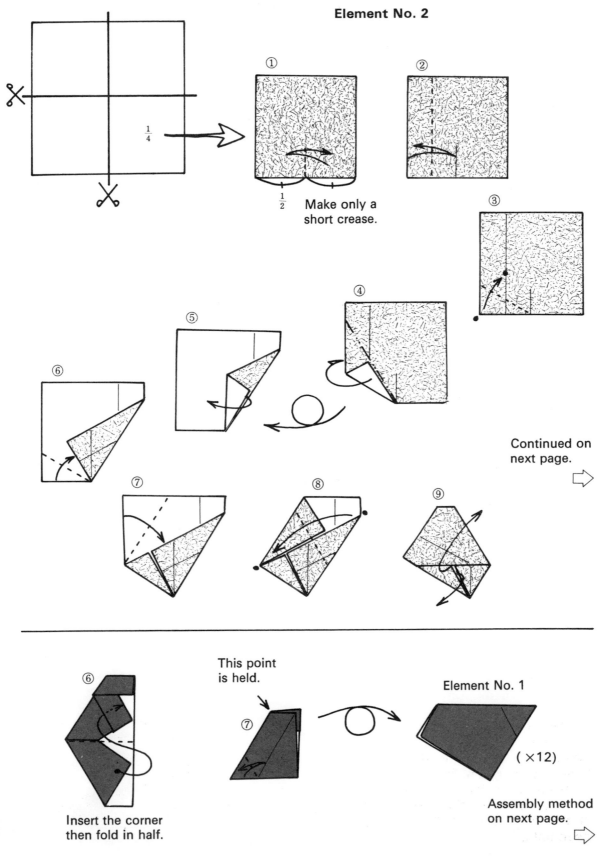

Element No. 2

$\frac{1}{4}$

① $\frac{1}{2}$ Make only a short crease.

②

③

④

⑤

⑥

⑦

⑧

⑨

Continued on next page.

⑥ Insert the corner then fold in half.

This point is held.

⑦

Element No. 1

(×12)

Assembly method on next page.

187

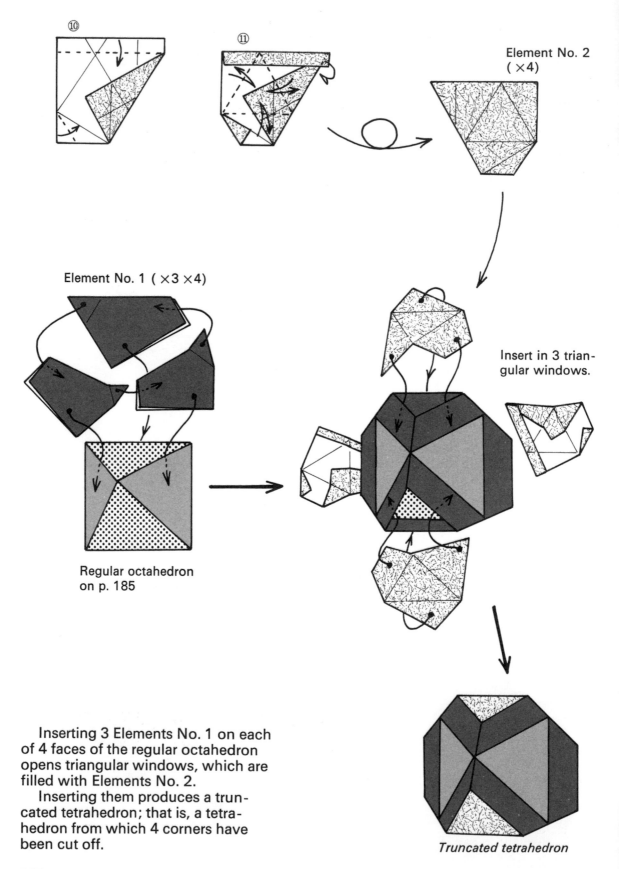

⑩

⑪

Element No. 2
(×4)

Element No. 1 (×3 ×4)

Insert in 3 triangular windows.

Regular octahedron
on p. 185

Inserting 3 Elements No. 1 on each
of 4 faces of the regular octahedron
opens triangular windows, which are
filled with Elements No. 2.

Inserting them produces a truncated tetrahedron; that is, a tetrahedron from which 4 corners have been cut off.

Truncated tetrahedron

Truncated Tetrahedron → Regular Tetrahedron

Element No. 3

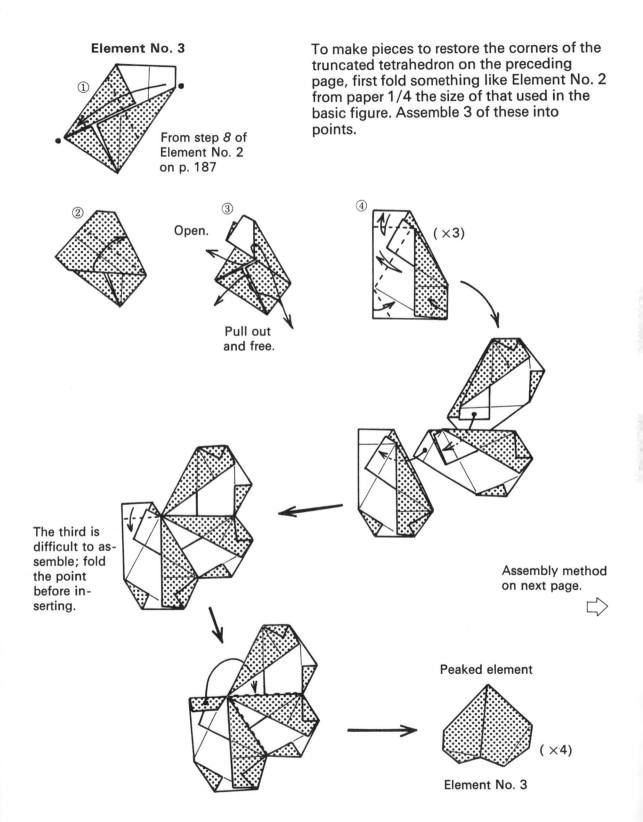

① From step *8* of Element No. 2 on p. 187

To make pieces to restore the corners of the truncated tetrahedron on the preceding page, first fold something like Element No. 2 from paper 1/4 the size of that used in the basic figure. Assemble 3 of these into points.

②

③ Open.

Pull out and free.

④ (×3)

The third is difficult to assemble; fold the point before inserting.

Assembly method on next page. ⇨

Peaked element

(×4)

Element No. 3

Element No. 3

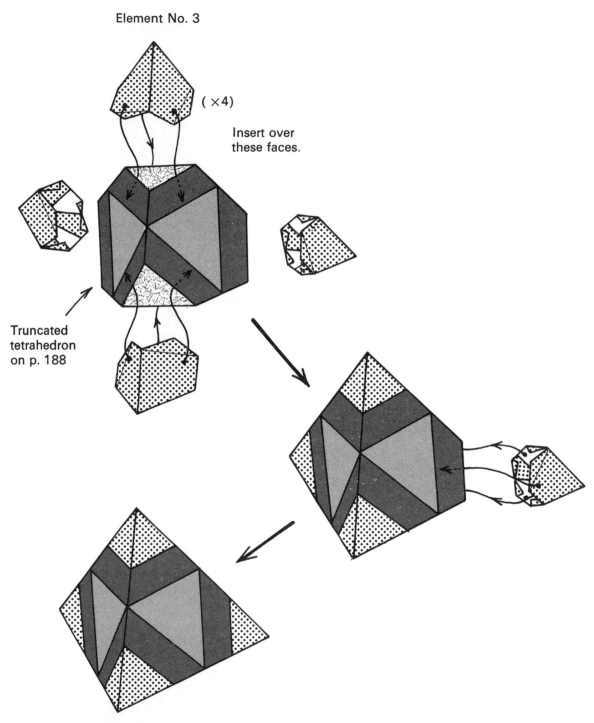

(×4)

Insert over these faces.

Truncated tetrahedron on p. 188

Regular tetrahedron

Though possessed of a distinctive beauty, as a geometric solid, the unadorned regular tetrahedron seems expressionless and unapproachable. Folding it this way with origami techniques, however, reveals its expressive eloquence, bares its secrets, and makes an interesting friend out of something that apparently offers nothing special.

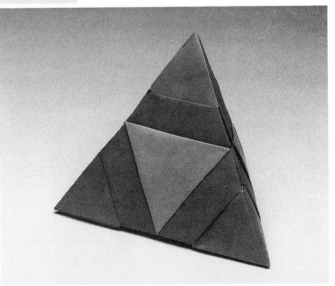

Transformation of Cuboctahedron III
Cuboctahedron → Truncated Hexahedron

In this third series of transformations of the cuboctahedron, the folding methods for many of the elements are uninteresting; but the brilliance emerges when they are inserted in the basic form. Use step *7* as a pattern for Element No. 1 and step *14* as a pattern for Element No. 2. For a labor-saving idea, refer to p. 145.

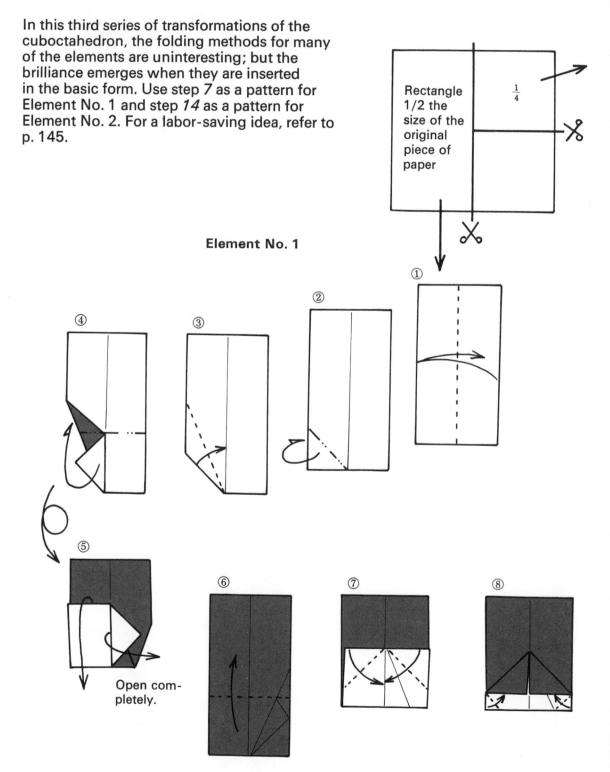

Rectangle 1/2 the size of the original piece of paper

$\frac{1}{4}$

Element No. 1

Open completely.

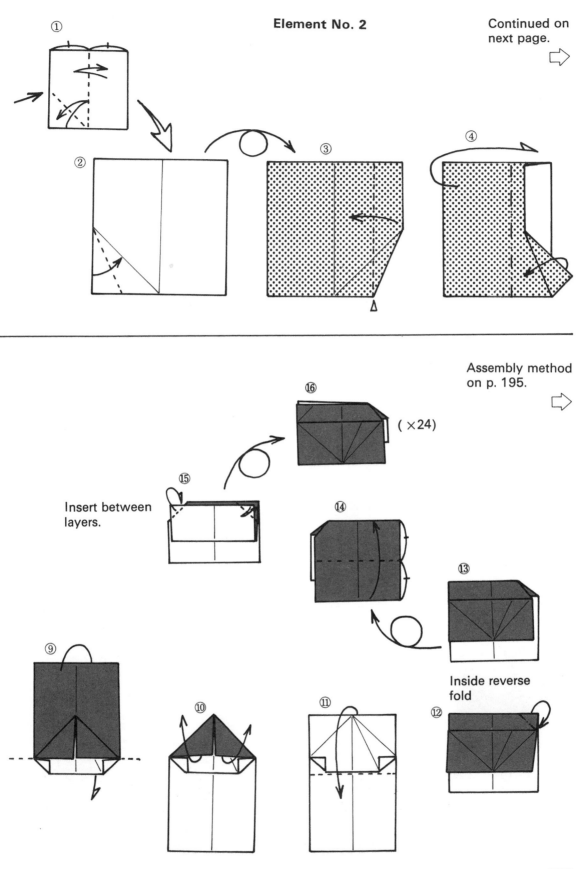

Element No. 2

Continued on next page. ⇨

① ② ③ ④

Assembly method on p. 195. ⇨

⑯ (×24)

⑮ Insert between layers.

⑭ ⑬

Inside reverse fold

⑨ ⑩ ⑪ ⑫

193

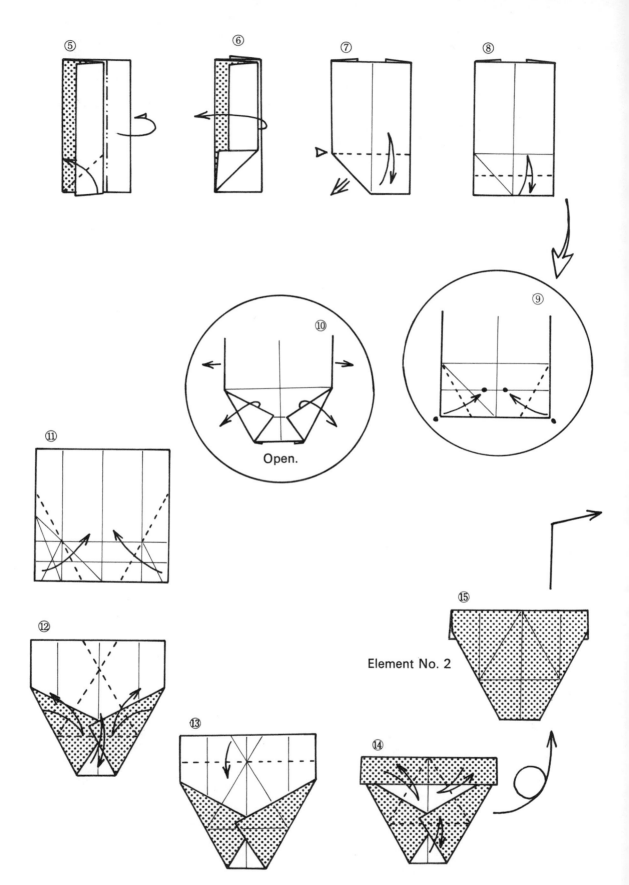

Open.

Element No. 2

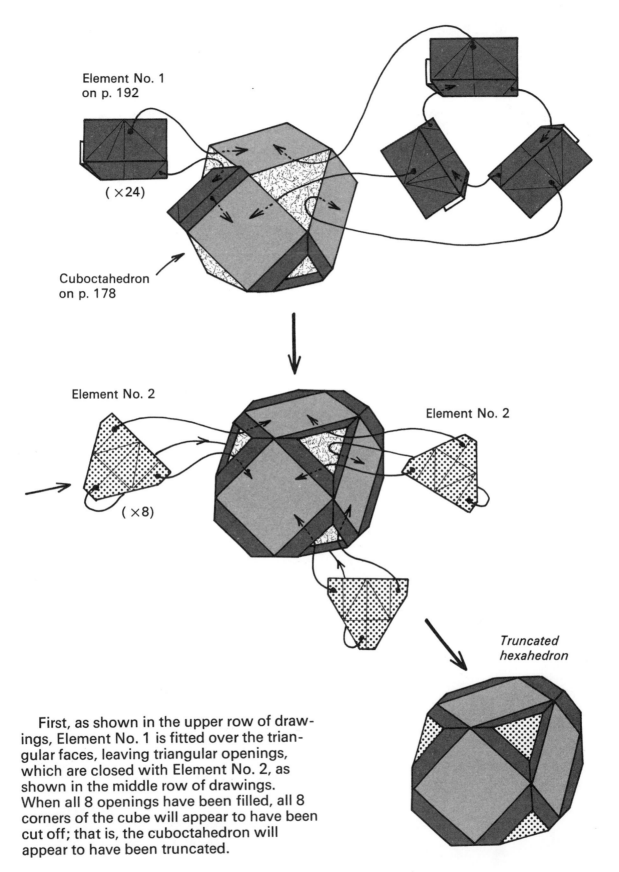

Element No. 1
on p. 192

(×24)

Cuboctahedron
on p. 178

Element No. 2

Element No. 2

(×8)

*Truncated
hexahedron*

First, as shown in the upper row of draw-ings, Element No. 1 is fitted over the trian-gular faces, leaving triangular openings, which are closed with Element No. 2, as shown in the middle row of drawings. When all 8 openings have been filled, all 8 corners of the cube will appear to have been cut off; that is, the cuboctahedron will appear to have been truncated.

Truncated Hexahedron → Cube → Compound Cube and Regular Octahedron

Now we shall restore corners to the truncated hexahedron. Make 8 of them and fit them over the triangular faces of the figure. And all of a sudden, a cube again! Next, fitting *G-a* over the square faces, make a compound cube and regular octahedron.

Element No. 3

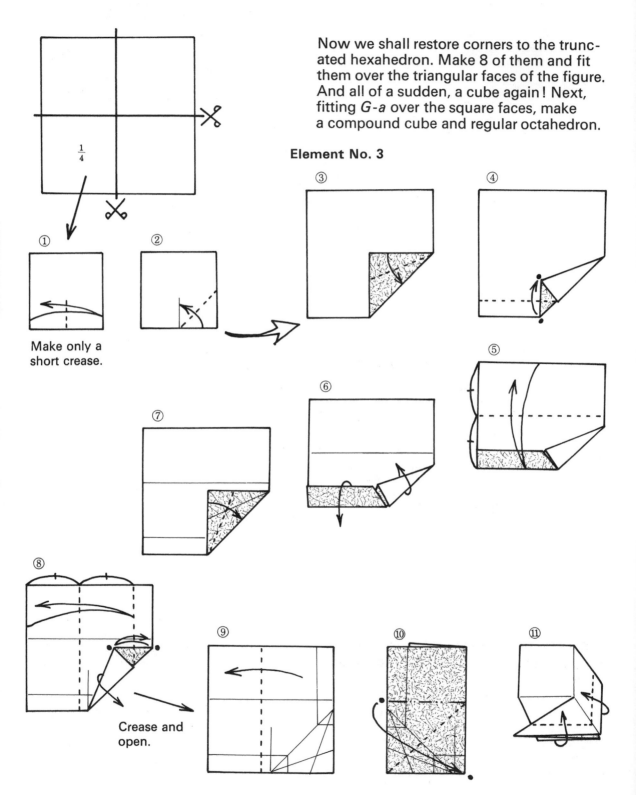

$\frac{1}{4}$

① Make only a short crease.

② Crease and open.

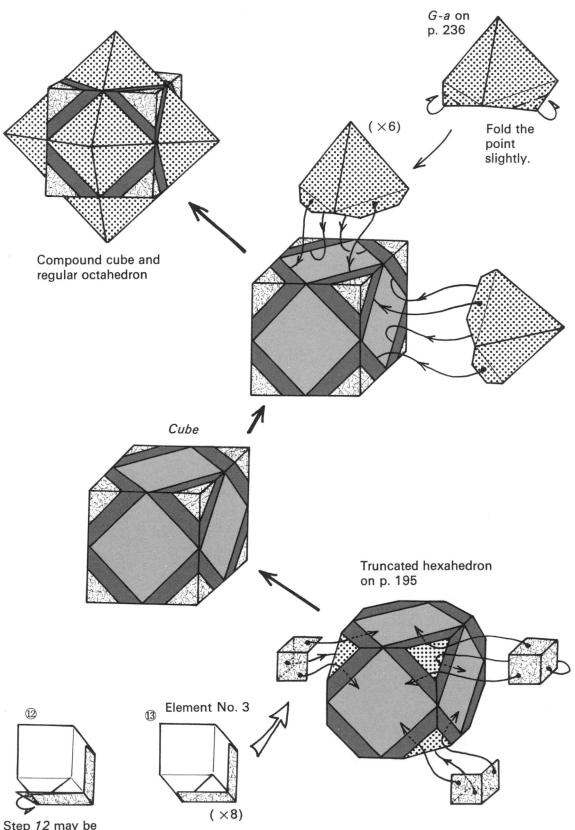

G-a on p. 236

Fold the point slightly.

(×6)

Compound cube and regular octahedron

Cube

Truncated hexahedron on p. 195

⑫

⑬ Element No. 3

(×8)

Step 12 may be folded or omitted.

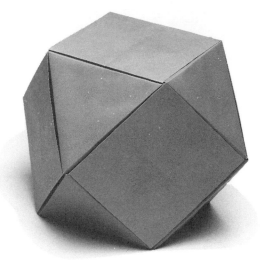

Cuboctahedron

Elements Nos. 1 and 2 convert the cuboctahedron on the left into a truncated hexahedron.

Various Transformations

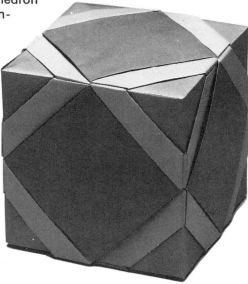

Elements No. 3 convert the truncated hexahedron into a cube.

Compound cube and regular octahedron

Transformation of Cuboctahedron IV
Cuboctahedron → Truncated Octahedron

The cuboctahedron on p. 178 is composed of square flat units. This transformation makes bases of the cuboctahedron on p. 182, which is composed of equilateral-triangular flat units. Because of the difference in location of the slits, their transformations are different.

First two elements are needed.

Element No. 1

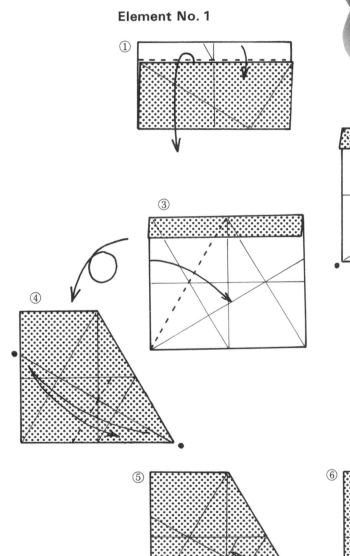

Continued on next page. ⇨

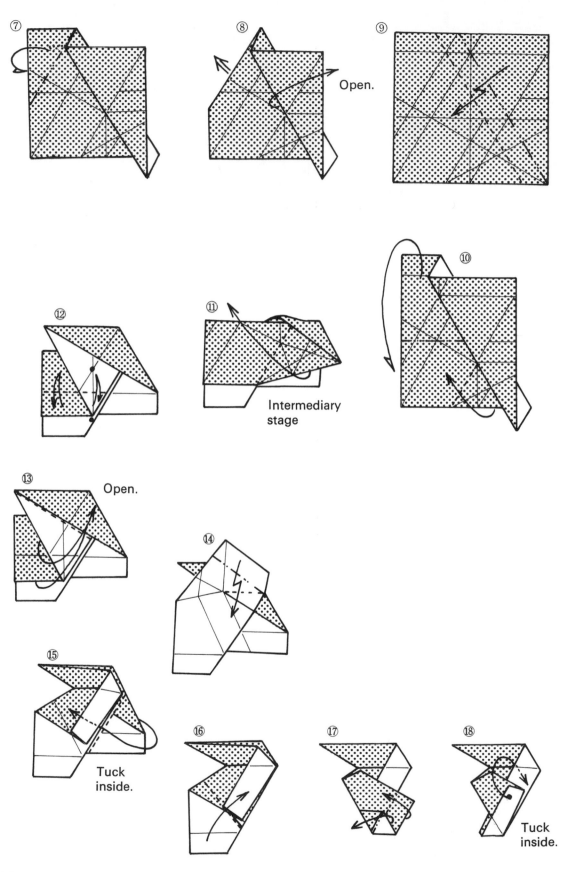

Open.

Intermediary
stage

Open.

Tuck
inside.

Tuck
inside.

Element No. 2

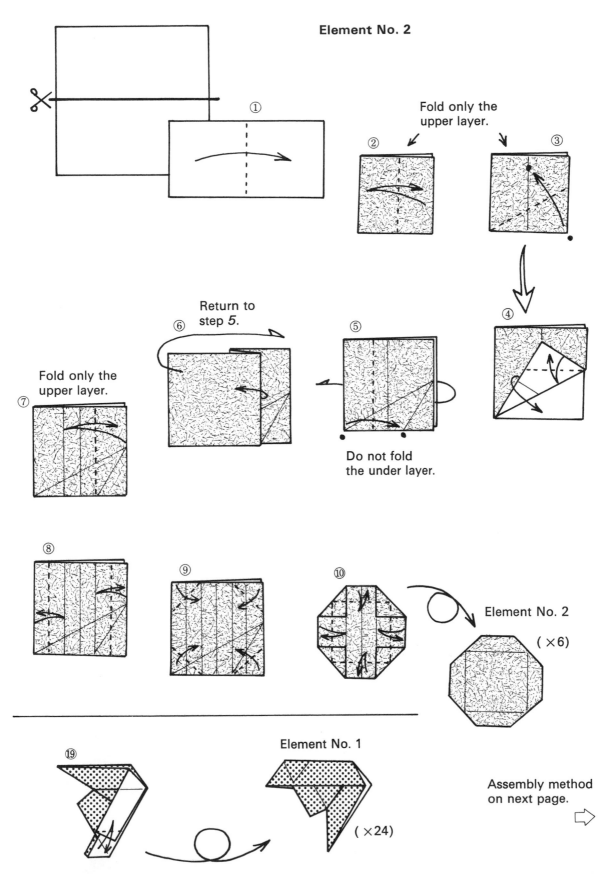

Fold only the upper layer.

① ② ③ ④

Return to step 5.

⑥ ⑤

Do not fold the under layer.

Fold only the upper layer.

⑦ ⑧ ⑨ ⑩

Element No. 2

(×6)

Element No. 1

⑲

(×24)

Assembly method on next page.

Adding these elements to a cuboctahedron
results in a truncated octahedron.

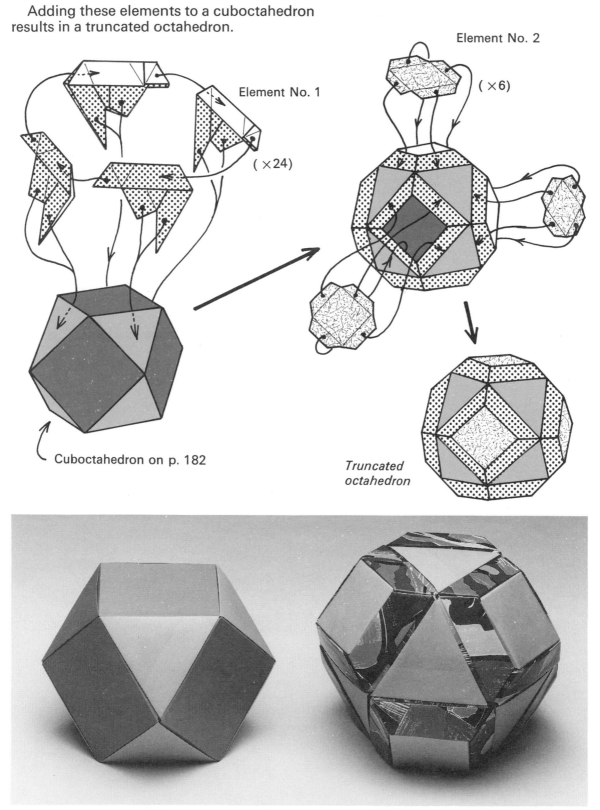

Element No. 1

(×24)

Element No. 2

(×6)

Cuboctahedron on p. 182

*Truncated
octahedron*

Adding Elements Nos. 1 and 2 to the cuboctahedron on the left produces the truncated
octahedron on the right.

Truncated Octahedron → Regular Octahedron

Element No. 3

Now we will fold elements to replace the truncated parts and restore the figure to a regular octahedron.

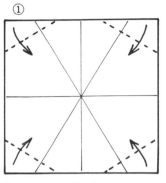

①

From step *10* of
F on p. 234

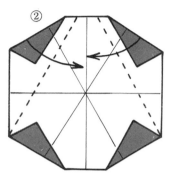

②

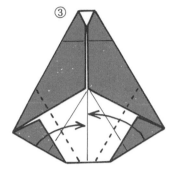

③

④

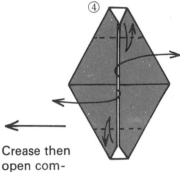

⑤

Crease then open completely.

⑥

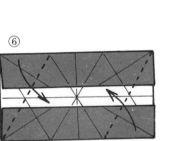

Continued on next page.

⑦

Crease then open completely.

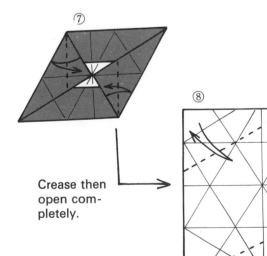

⑧

⑨

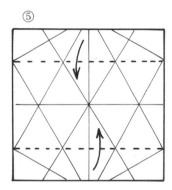

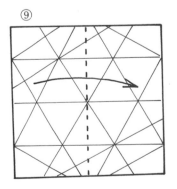

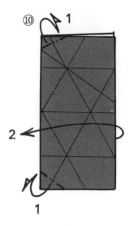

⑩

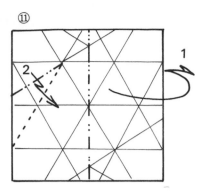

⑪

2

1

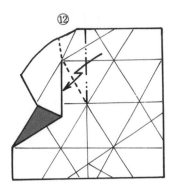

⑫

Pull out.

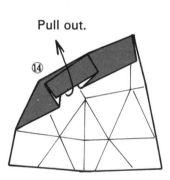

⑭

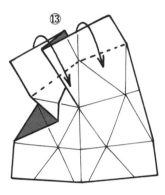

⑬

Partial enlargement

⑮

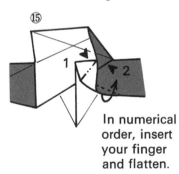

1   2

In numerical
order, insert
your finger
and flatten.

⑯

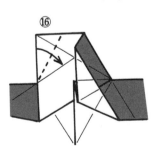

⑰

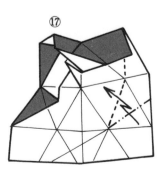

⑱

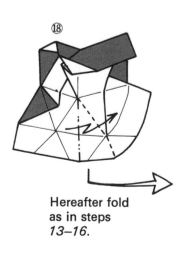

Hereafter fold
as in steps
13–16.

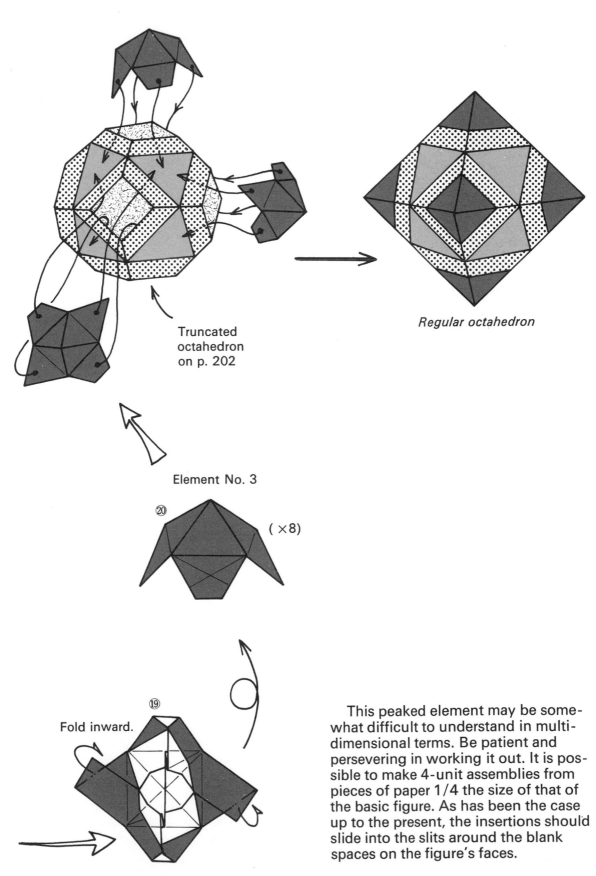

Truncated
octahedron
on p. 202

Regular octahedron

Element No. 3

⑳   (×8)

⑲

Fold inward.

This peaked element may be some-
what difficult to understand in multi-
dimensional terms. Be patient and
persevering in working it out. It is possible to make 4-unit assemblies from
pieces of paper 1/4 the size of that of
the basic figure. As has been the case
up to the present, the insertions should
slide into the slits around the blank
spaces on the figure's faces.

Regular Octahedron → Compound Cube and Regular Octahedron

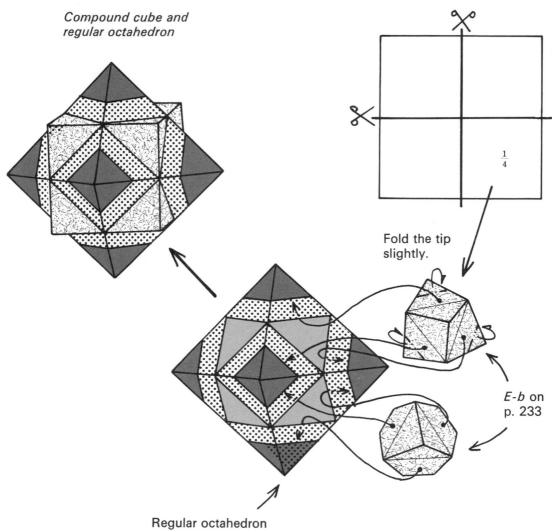

Compound cube and
regular octahedron

$\frac{1}{4}$

Fold the tip
slightly.

E-b on
p. 233

Regular octahedron
on p. 205

The thickness of the paper makes the finished figure look a little plump and heavy. You may alter the size of the paper to rectify this situation. But it seems to me that, since the important characteristic of origami is ease and convenience, we ought to be able to overlook slight visual shortcomings. Gradually removing the outer additional elements to reveal the figures inside is a source of surprise and enjoyment even to the person who folded the figure and knows perfectly what comes next. People who do not know are likely to be kept sitting on the edges of their chairs in pleasurable surprise and anticipation.

Truncated
octahedron
(p. 202)

Truncated octahedron
plus Elements No. 3 pro-
duces a regular octa-
hedron.

Regular octahedron
plus *E-b* produces a compound cube and
regular octahedron.

Small Square Flat Unit

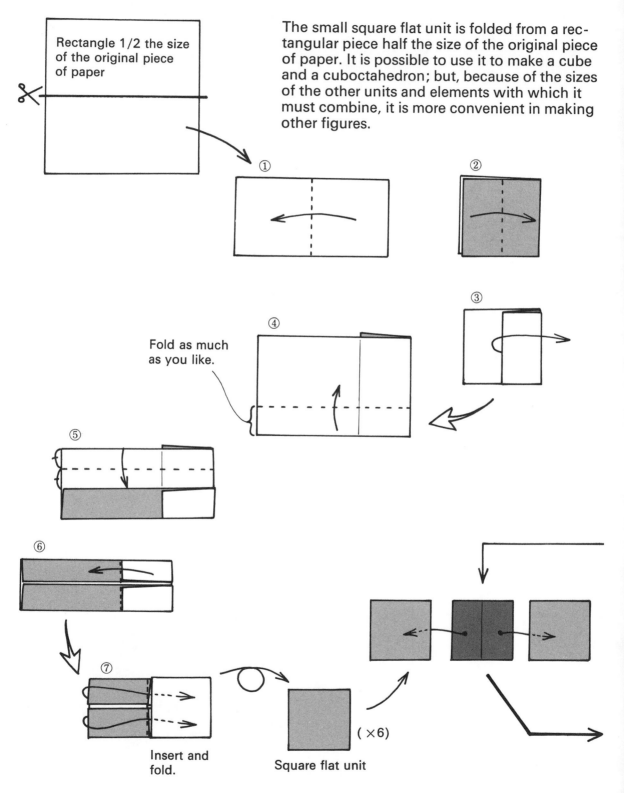

Rectangle 1/2 the size of the original piece of paper

The small square flat unit is folded from a rectangular piece half the size of the original piece of paper. It is possible to use it to make a cube and a cuboctahedron; but, because of the sizes of the other units and elements with which it must combine, it is more convenient in making other figures.

① ② ③

Fold as much as you like.

④ ⑤ ⑥ ⑦

Insert and fold.

Square flat unit

(×6)

Cube before final assembly (left) and after final assembly (right)

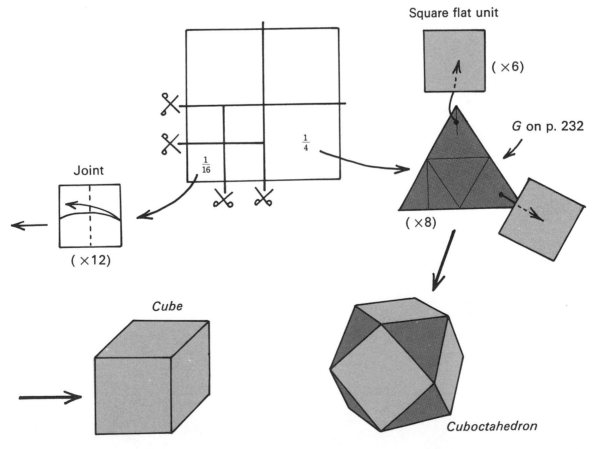

Square flat unit

(×6)

G on p. 232

(×8)

Joint

(×12)

$\frac{1}{16}$

$\frac{1}{4}$

Cube

Cuboctahedron

Transformation of Rhombicuboctahedron

The rhombicuboctahedron is the basic figure in this section. Elements Nos. 1 and 2 are combined with the small square flat units.

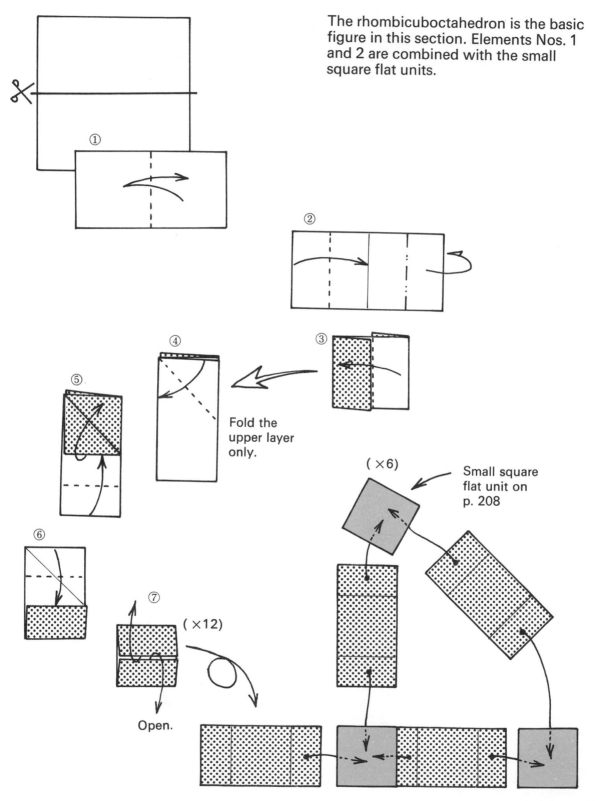

①

②

③

④

Fold the upper layer only.

⑤

⑥

⑦

Open.

(×12)

(×6)

Small square flat unit on p. 208

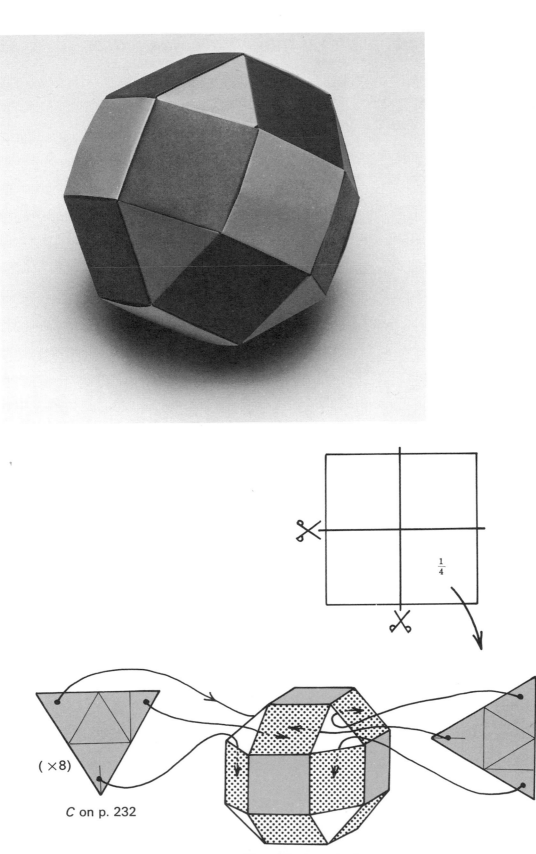

$\frac{1}{4}$

(×8)

C on p. 232

Rhombicuboctahedron

Rhombicuboctahedron → Truncated Hexahedron

Element No. 1

A complete transformation of the rhombicuboctahedron into another solid requires 3 additional elements. But the intermediary phase produced by appending only Element No. 1 is interesting.

Use step 7 as a pattern for Element No. 1 to save labor.

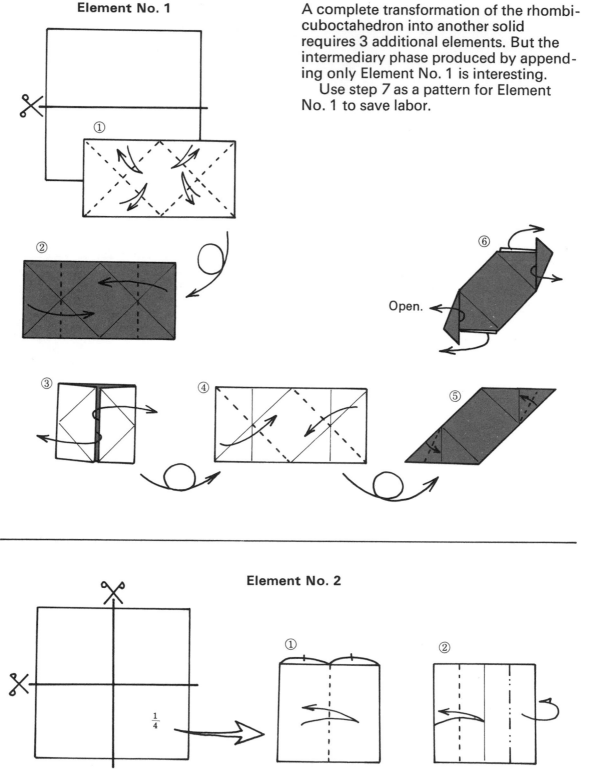

Open.

Element No. 2

$\frac{1}{4}$

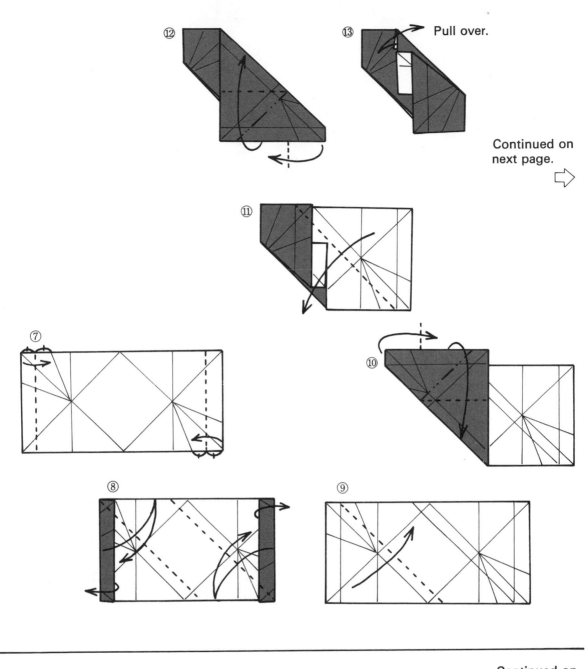

⑫

⑬ Pull over.

Continued on
next page.
⇨

⑪

⑦

⑩

⑧

⑨

Continued on
next page.
⇨

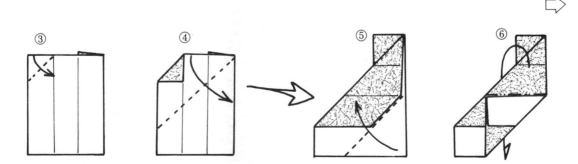

③

④

⑤

⑥

213

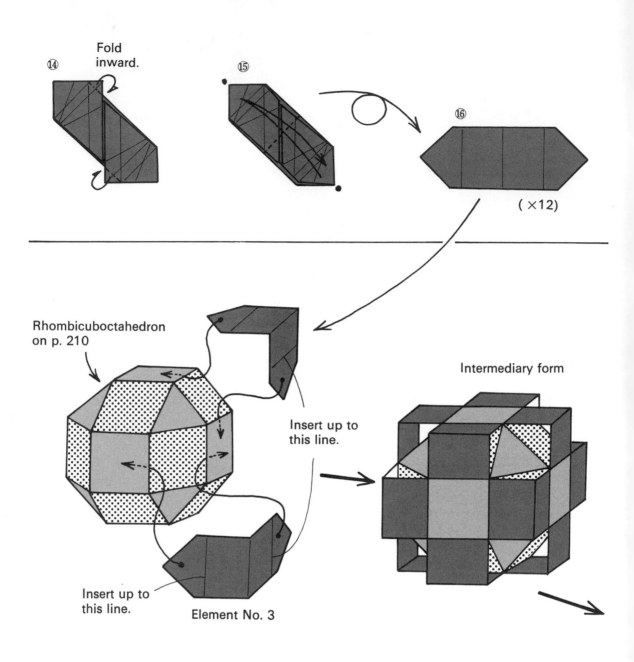

⑭ Fold inward.

⑮

⑯

(×12)

Rhombicuboctahedron on p. 210

Intermediary form

Insert up to this line.

Insert up to this line.

Element No. 3

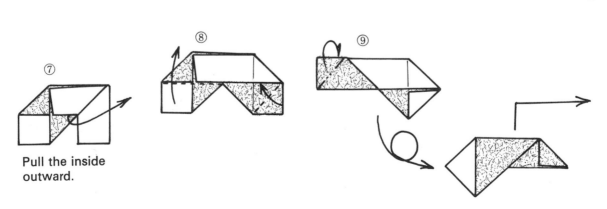

⑦

Pull the inside outward.

⑧

⑨

Element No. 3

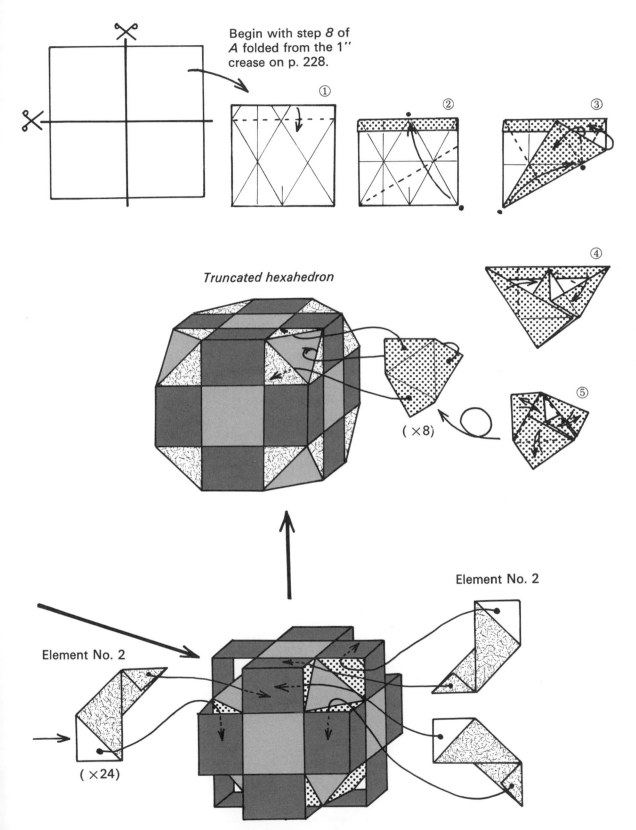

Begin with step *8* of
A folded from the 1''
crease on p. 228.

①

②

③

④

Truncated hexahedron

(×8)

⑤

Element No. 2

Element No. 2

(×24)

215

Truncated Hexahedron → Cube

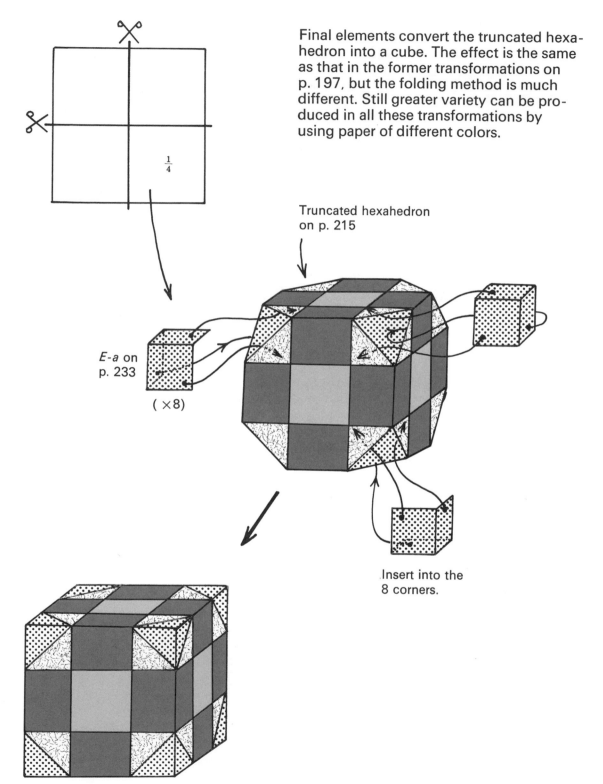

Final elements convert the truncated hexahedron into a cube. The effect is the same as that in the former transformations on p. 197, but the folding method is much different. Still greater variety can be produced in all these transformations by using paper of different colors.

$\frac{1}{4}$

Truncated hexahedron on p. 215

E-a on p. 233

(×8)

Insert into the 8 corners.

Cube

Rhombicuboctahedron

Rhombicuboctahedron plus Elements No. 1

The figure in the lower right plus *D* produces a cube.

The figure above plus Elements Nos. 2 and 3 produces a truncated hexahedron.

Square and Equilateral-triangular Flat Units from Rectangles

Square flat unit

Origami is not limited to square paper. The propeller unit on p. 124 is folded from triangular paper; and it is possible to produce square and equilateral-triangular flat units from rectangular pieces of paper. If you begin with pieces of paper of the same size, the bases of the 2 completed flat units will be the same length.

①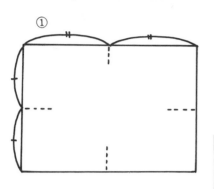

② ③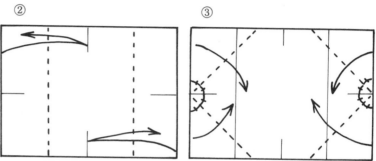

④

⑥ 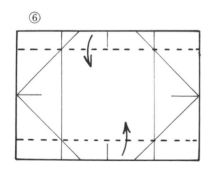 ⑤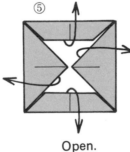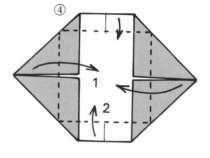

Open.

⑦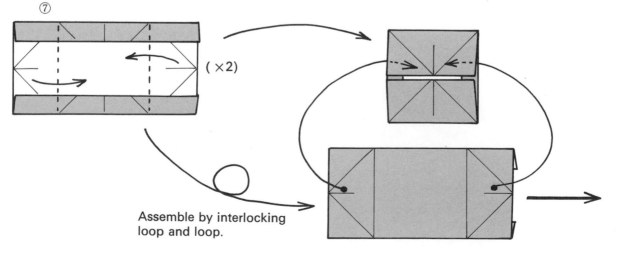

(×2)

Assemble by interlocking loop and loop.

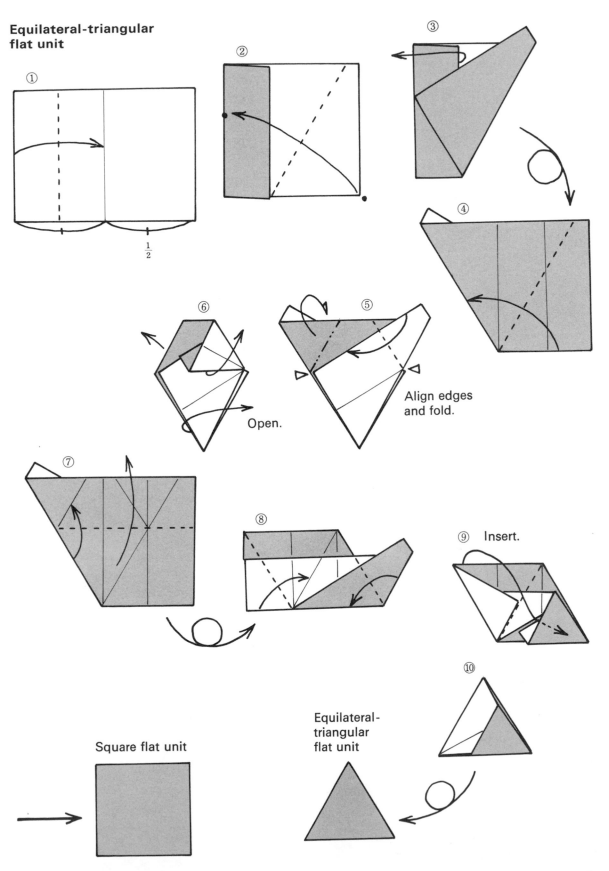

Equilateral-triangular flat unit

① ② ③ ④ ⑤

Align edges and fold.

⑥ Open.

⑦ ⑧ ⑨ Insert.

⑩

Square flat unit

Equilateral-triangular flat unit

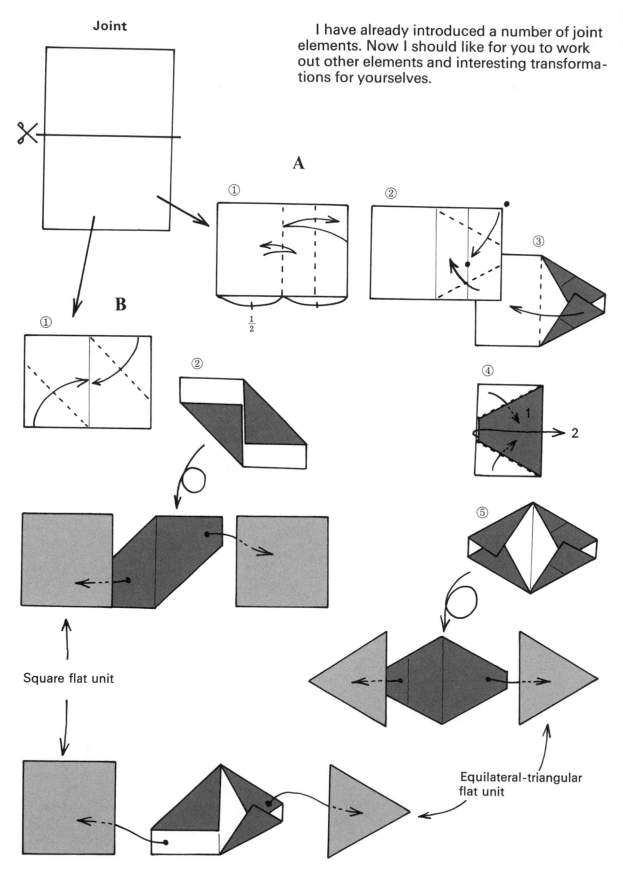

Joint

I have already introduced a number of joint elements. Now I should like for you to work out other elements and interesting transformations for yourselves.

A

① ② ③

$\frac{1}{2}$

④

1

2

⑤

B

① ②

Square flat unit

Equilateral-triangular flat unit

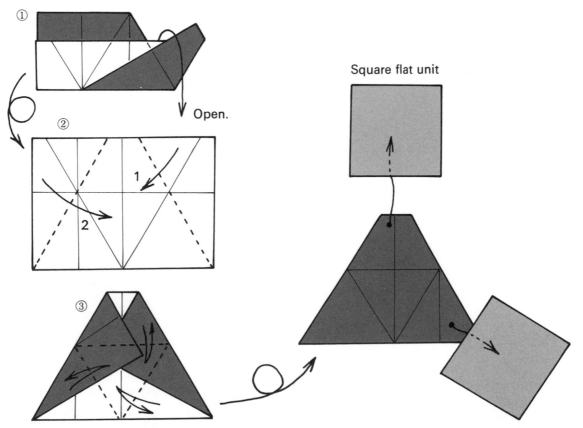

From step *8* on p. 219

①

② Open.

③

Square flat unit

Regular-hexagonal Flat Unit

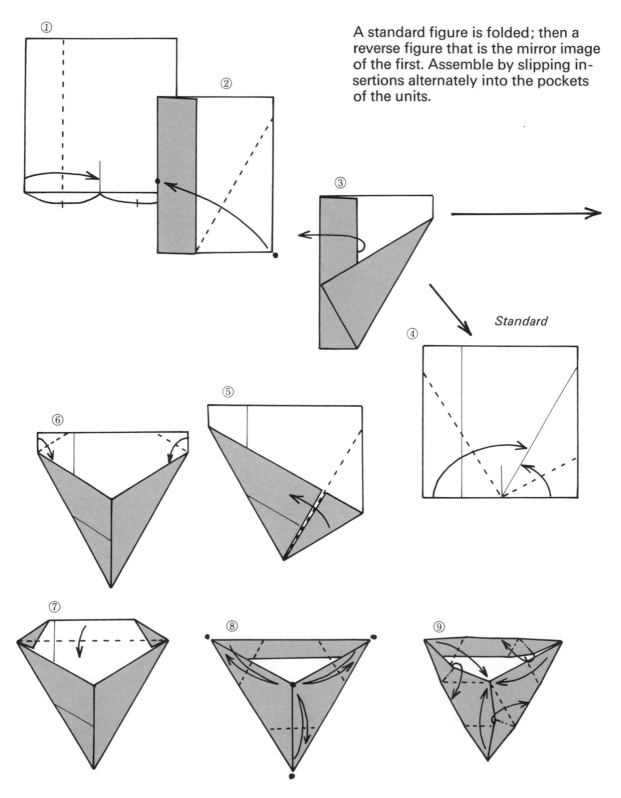

A standard figure is folded; then a reverse figure that is the mirror image of the first. Assemble by slipping insertions alternately into the pockets of the units.

Standard

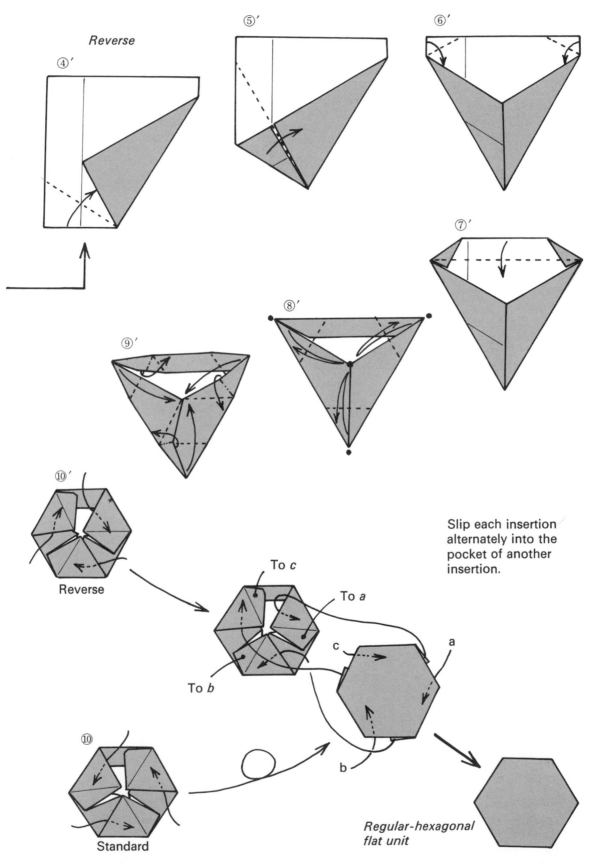

Reverse

④′

⑤′

⑥′

⑦′

⑧′

⑨′

⑩′

Reverse

To *c*

To *a*

c

a

To *b*

b

Slip each insertion
alternately into the
pocket of another
insertion.

⑩

Standard

*Regular-hexagonal
flat unit*

Joint

Regular-hexagonal flat units are combined with joints, leaving triangular or square windows which are then filled with elements. Of course, these may be assembled in plane forms as shown on p. 55.

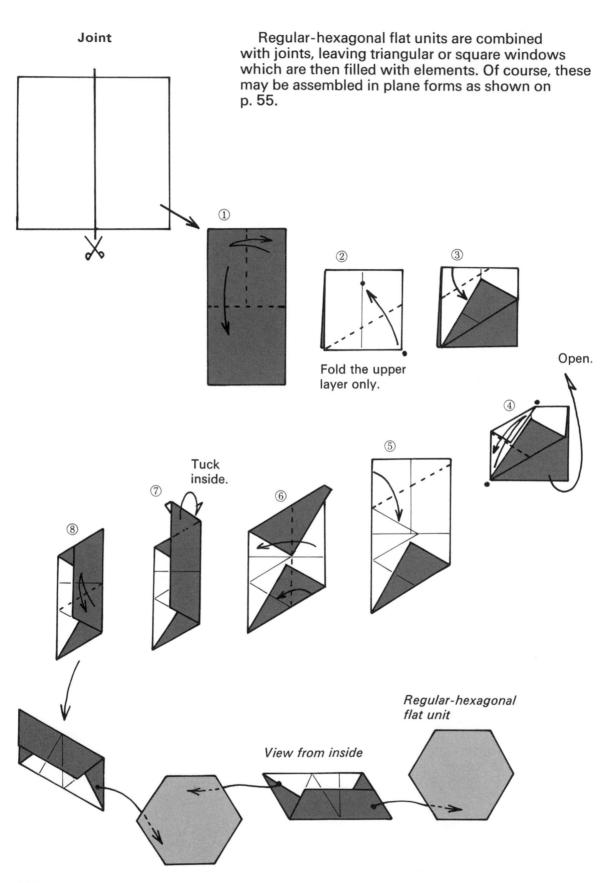

①

② Fold the upper layer only.

③

④ Open.

⑤

⑥

⑦ Tuck inside.

⑧

Regular-hexagonal flat unit

View from inside

Variation

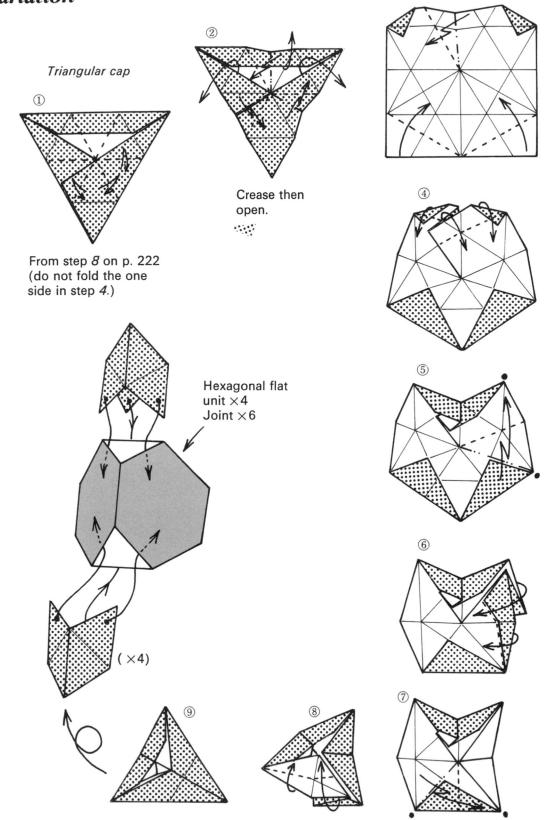

Triangular cap

①

②

Crease then
open.

③

④

⑤

⑥

⑦

⑧

⑨

From step *8* on p. 222
(do not fold the one
side in step *4.*)

Hexagonal flat
unit ×4
Joint ×6

(×4)

225

Square cap

①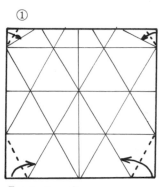

From step *3*
on p. 225

②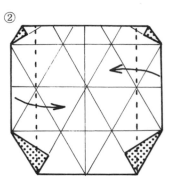

③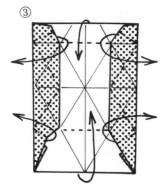

④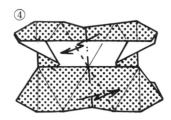

⑤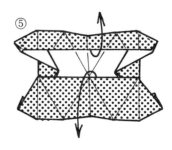

⑥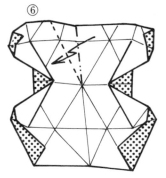

⑦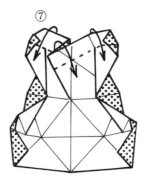

⑧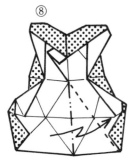

⑨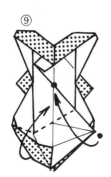

⑩

Hexagonal flat unit ×8
Joint ×12

(×6)

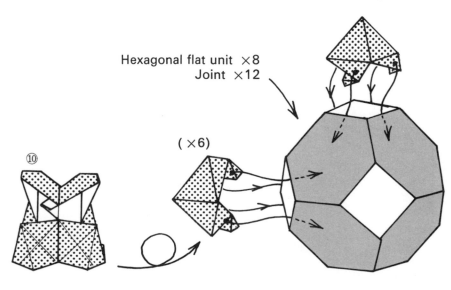

Three solid figures made from hexagonal flat units and triangular-cap units

Adding square-cap units to the solid on the left produces the solid on the right.

Examples of 60° Folding

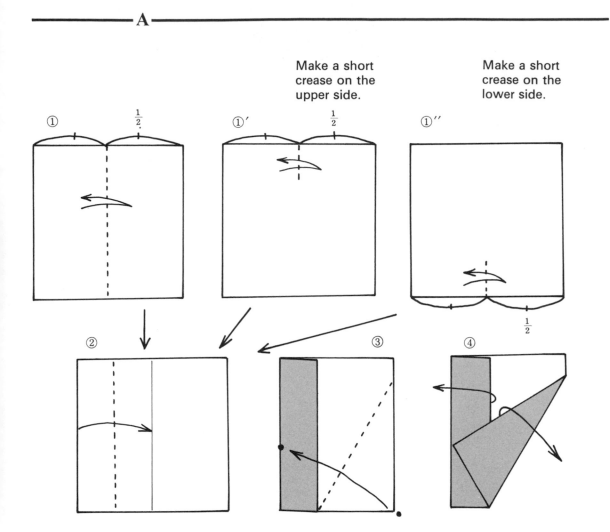

Make a short crease on the upper side.

Make a short crease on the lower side.

The Finishing must be Careful and Neat

A and *B* show 2 ways of producing the 60° angles that are essential in making equilateral triangles. Since the end results of both are the same, it might seem that a single way would suffice. But sometimes using both makes for cleaner, neater finishing. It is demanding but very important to finish origami so that no unnecessary creases appear on the exposed surfaces, so that the form is immediately understandable and recognizable, and so that the whole thing is pleasing to look at.

This is why in devising origami folds I first work to produce the form I have in mind and then rework to eliminate unwanted creases. To do this, I unfold the finished unit and examine all the creases appearing on the exposed surface to determine whether some of them might not be done away with. If this does not produce the degree of neatness I want, I start all over and try to think up new, different units.

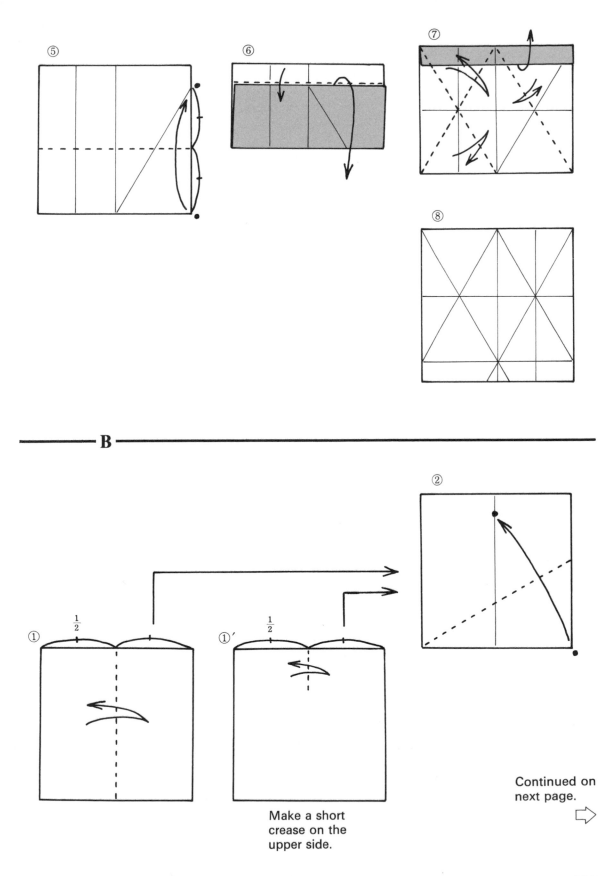

⑤

⑥

⑦

⑧

B

① $\frac{1}{2}$

①′ $\frac{1}{2}$

Make a short
crease on the
upper side.

②

Continued on
next page.

⇨

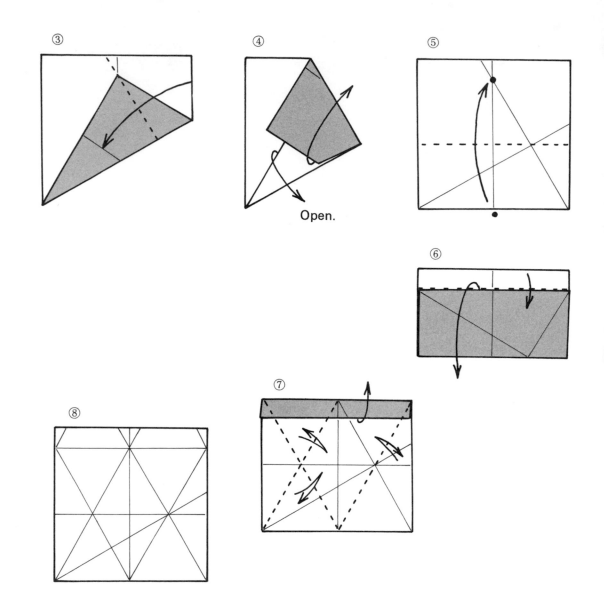

Open.

In the case of these 2 examples, the process is troublesome; but the finished result is beautiful. That is excellent. But I often cannot make up my mind whether to put beauty or ease of folding first because sometimes, folds that are lovely when finished are hard to produce and therefore unstable and likely to cause mistakes. Even in such instances, practice makes perfect. Folding and refolding something that is not easy eliminate much of the trouble and insecurity. But familiarity can breed contempt, and whether facility gained through repeated practice is necessarily good depends on the case in hand.

When all is said and done, I strive for clear, interesting folding order, clean finish, and the achievement of goals I set myself. If I fall short of my goal, I demand to know why.

230

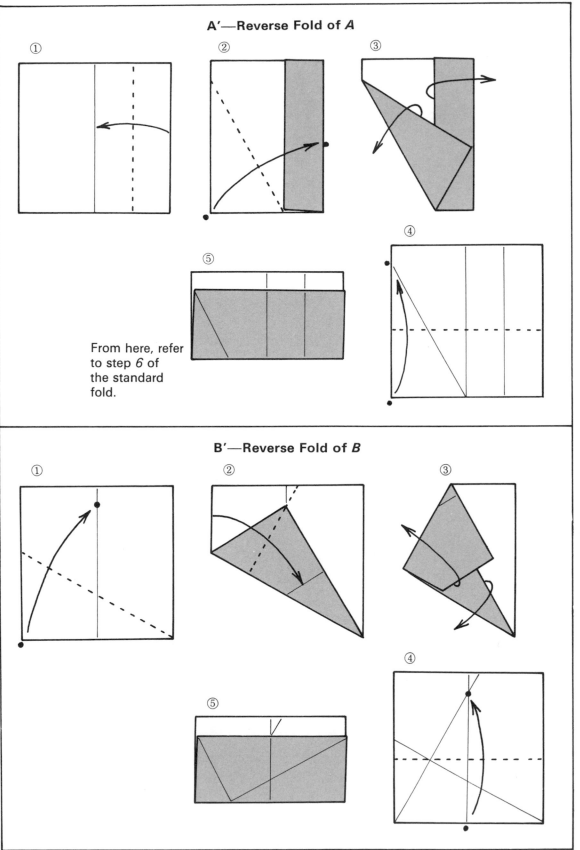

A'—Reverse Fold of A

① ② ③

From here, refer to step *6* of the standard fold.

⑤ ④

B'—Reverse Fold of B

① ② ③

⑤ ④

Folding Elements

Here, in one location, are several of the most widely used elements arranged in alphabetical order, beginning on p. 228.

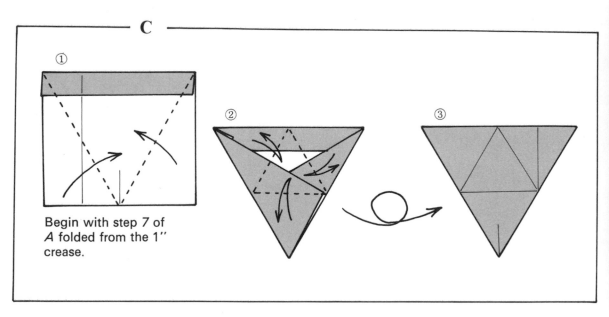

C

① Begin with step 7 of *A* folded from the 1″ crease.

②

③

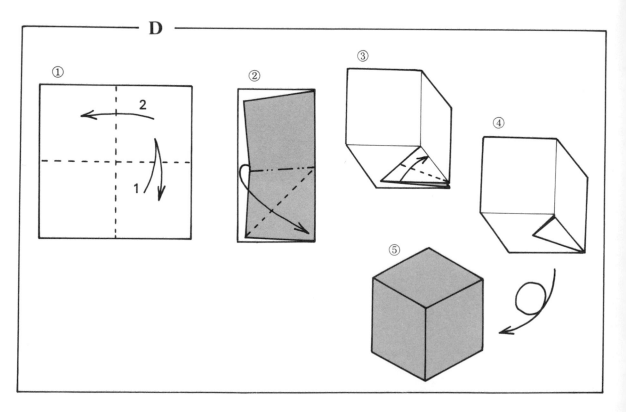

D

①

②

③

④

⑤

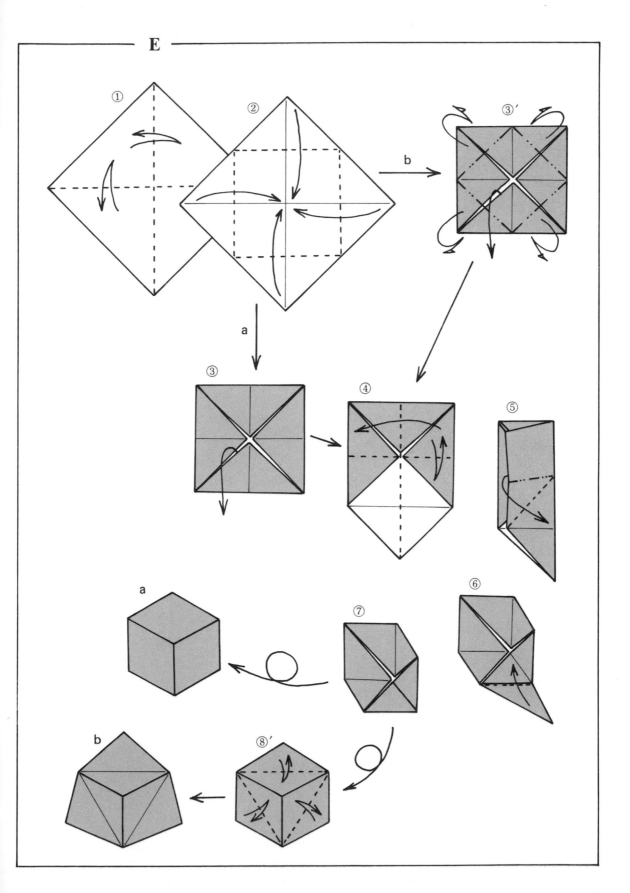

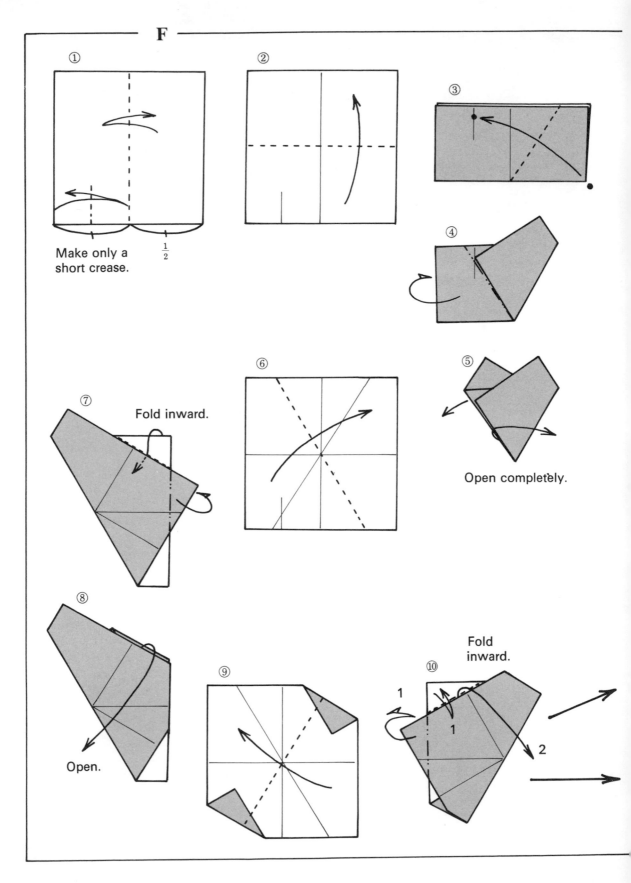

F

① Make only a
short crease.

$\frac{1}{2}$

②

③

④

⑤ Open completely.

⑥

⑦ Fold inward.

⑧ Open.

⑨

⑩ Fold
inward.

1

1

2

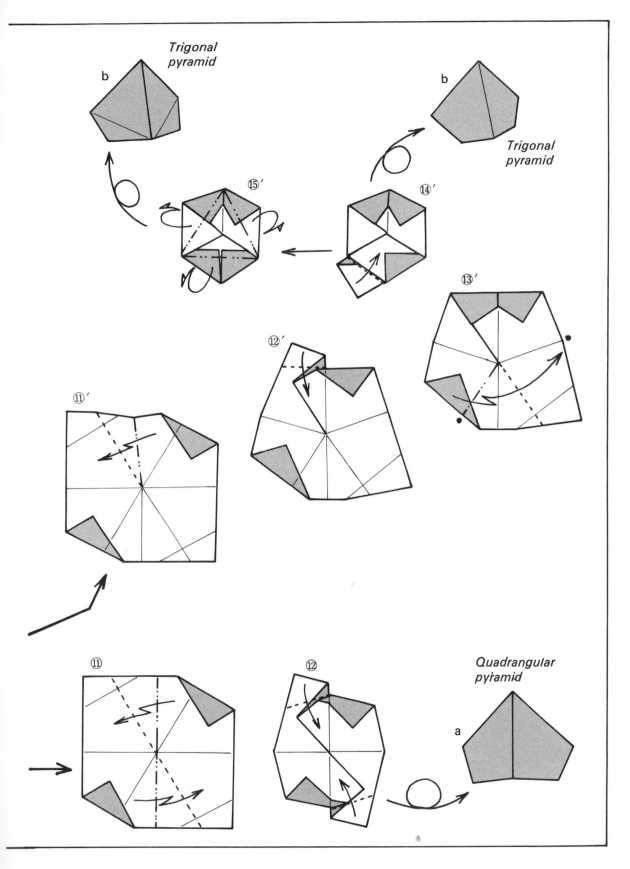

Trigonal pyramid

b

b

Trigonal pyramid

⑮′

⑭′

⑬′

⑪′

⑫′

⑪

⑫

Quadrangular pyramid

a

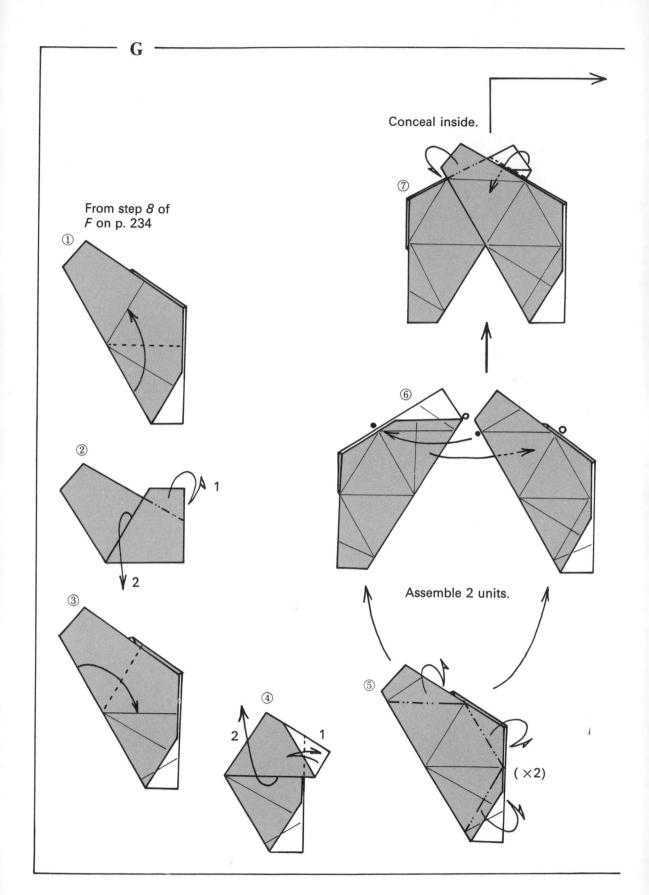

Conceal inside.

⑦

From step *8* of
F on p. 234

①

②

1

2

③

④

2

1

⑤

(×2)

⑥

Assemble 2 units.

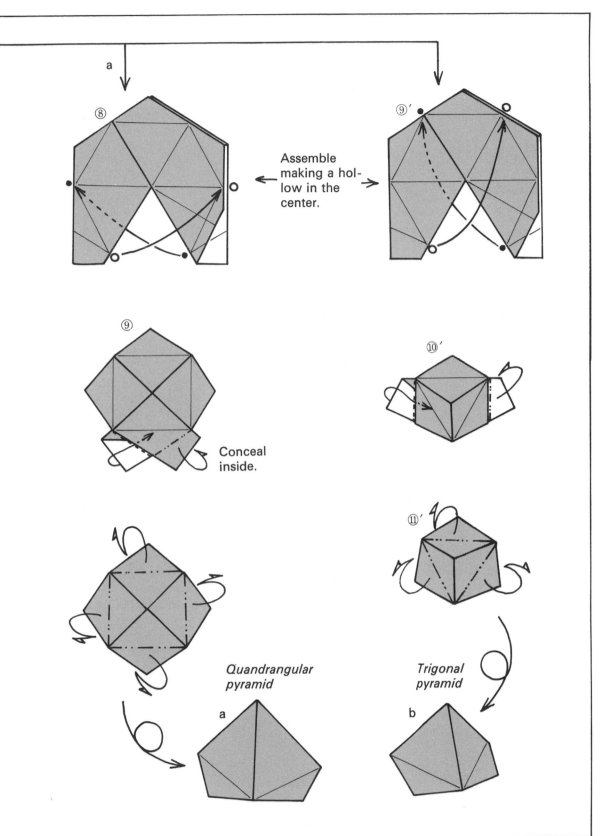

a

⑧

Assemble
making a hol-
low in the
center.

⑨′

⑨

Conceal
inside.

⑩′

⑪′

*Quandrangular
pyramid*

a

*Trigonal
pyramid*

b

Polyhedrons Summarized

No.	Polyhedrons	Shape and Numbers of Surfaces	Surfaces	Apexes	Edges
1	Regular tetrahedron	△ ×4	4	4	6
2	Hexahedron (cube)	□ ×6	6	8	12
3	Octahedron	△ ×8	8	6	12
4	Dodecahedron	⬠ ×12	12	20	30
5	Icosahedron	△ ×20	20	12	30
6	Truncated tetrahedron	△ ×4 ⬡ ×4	8	12	18
7	Truncated hexahedron	△ ×8 ⯄ ×6	14	24	36
8	Truncated octahedron	□ ×6 ⬡ ×8	14	24	36
9	Truncated dodecahedron	△ ×20 ⯄ ×12	32	60	90
10	Truncated icosahedron	⬠ ×12 ⬡ ×20	32	60	90
11	Cuboctahedron	△ ×8 □ ×6	14	12	24
12	Icosidodecahedron	△ ×20 ⬠ ×12	32	30	60
13	Rhombicuboctahedron	△ ×8 □ ×18	26	24	48
14	Rhombitruncated cuboctahedron	□ ×12 ⬡ ×8 ⯄ ×6	26	48	72
15	Rhombicosidodeca-hedron	△ ×20 □ ×30 ⬠ ×12	62	60	120
16	Rhombitruncated icosidodecahedron	□ ×30 ⬡ ×20 ⯄ ×12	62	120	180
17	Snub cube	△ ×32 □ ×6	38	24	60
18	Snub dodecahedron	△ ×80 ⬠ ×12	92	60	150

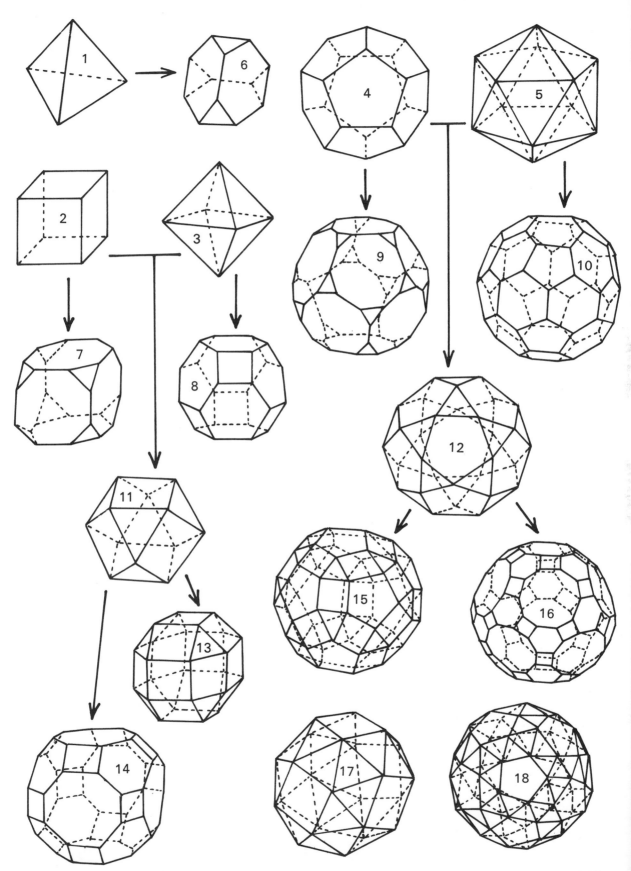

Index